KINtop Studies in Early Cinema – volume 1
series editors: Frank Kessler, Sabine Lenk, Martin Loiperdinger

Early Cinema Today:
The Art of
Programming and
Live Performance

KINtop. Studies in Early Cinema

KINtop Studies in Early Cinema expands the efforts to promote historical research and theoretical reflection on the emergence of moving pictures undertaken by the internationally acclaimed *KINtop* yearbook (published in German from 1992–2006). It brings a new collection of anthologies and monographs in English by internationally renowned authors as well as young scholars. The scope of the series ranges from studies on the formative years of the emerging medium of animated photographs to research on the institution-alisation of cinema in the years up to the First World War. Books in this series will also explore the many facets of 19th and early 20th century visual culture as well as initiatives to preserve and present this cinematographic heritage. Early cinema has become one of the most dynamic fields of scholarly research in cinema studies worldwide, and this series aims to provide an international platform for new insights and fresh discoveries in this thriving area.

Series editors: Frank Kessler, Sabine Lenk and Martin Loiperdinger

Early Cinema Today:
The Art of
Programming and
Live Performance

Edited by
Martin Loiperdinger

British Library Cataloguing in Publication Data

Early Cinema Today:
The Art of Programming and Live Performance

Series: KINtop Studies in Early Cinema – volume 1

A catalogue entry for this book is available from the British Library

ISBN: 9780 86196 702 5 (Paperback)

Published by
John Libbey Publishing Ltd, 3 Leicester Road, New Barnet, Herts EN5 5EW, United Kingdom
e-mail: john.libbey@orange.fr; web site: www.johnlibbey.com
Direct orders (UK and Europe): direct.orders@marston.co.uk

Distributed in N. America by **Indiana University Press**, 601 North Morton St,
Bloomington, IN 47404, USA. www.iupress.indiana.edu

Printed and bound in China by 1010 Printing International Ltd.

Contents

Martin Loiperdinger

Preface

Early cinema and its media performance practices had already fallen into oblivion for more than six decades when the International Federation of Film Archives (FIAF) screened fiction films from 1900 to 1906 to film scholars and archivists at the now legendary Brighton conference in 1978. The first steps to be taken following this initiative, of course, were to examine and study the material itself, i.e. the artefacts from that early period which the film archives kept in unmarked tin cans. The next steps then were to do research on the production, distribution, exhibition and reception of those artefacts, i.e. to reconstruct different aspects of early cinema history. In this respect, the Nederlands Filmmuseum (NFM, now named EYE – Film Institute Netherlands) became one of the leading archives because it had shown foresight in undertaking preservation and research efforts which afforded access to its rich collections from the first decades of the 20th century – mainly the Desmet collection – to the international research community. The two Amsterdam Workshops on *Non-fiction from the 1910s* (1994) and on *Disorderly Order – Colours in Silent Film* (1995), both curated by Daan Hertogs and Niko de Klerk, were eye-openers: the beautiful prints and their efficient programming were a surprise for everybody present who was not yet familiar with the marvellous collections of the Nederlands Filmmuseum.

In subsequent years, programming early cinema, for professional as well as for non-professional audiences, became an issue. Audiences also became an issue on various occasions. This first volume of *KINtop – Studies in Early Cinema* aims to provide first-hand insights given by the curators of some groundbreaking endeavours in arranging early cinema performances in Italy, Belgium, Great Britain, Germany and Luxemburg.

Starting in 2003, the regular retrospective *100 Years Ago* at the Cinema Ritrovato festival in Bologna became the annual focus of early cinema presentation, showing about ten carefully composed programmes of the respective year's film production of just a century ago. Owing to the outstanding sensitivity which Mariann Lewinsky has been devoting to the curation of this retrospective since 2004, Bologna is unquestionably the best place to represent the wide and lively range and colourful richness which early cinema programmes can offer. Accordingly, Mariann Lewinsky's contribution to this volume describes, from her personal point of view, how she composes her film programmes, somehow comparable to a multi-course gourmet meal. Recently, in collaboration with Eric de Kuyper, she curated the ten programmes of the retrospective *From the Deep: The Experimental Film 1898–1918* at the International Short Film Festival Oberhausen, in 2010. Tom Gunning, in his review of this major early cinema event, most notably underlines the "delight in variety and sudden juxtapositions" which many young filmmakers among the audience were offered to experience. The Oberhausen festival was the right place for the retrospective because, a century ago, indeed many filmmakers undertook experiments in what the new medium could do (if without claiming to be avant-garde artists).

Besides these comprehensive retrospectives the last decade saw some elaborate examples of programming early films on special topics to present a collection, to investigate a subject or to arouse special interest in chosen audiences for early films. There were Nico de Klerk's Biograph programmes and Vanessa Toulmin's Mitchell & Kenyon programmes which presented samples of the surviving film production of these companies to the professional audience of Le Giornate del Cinema Muto in Pordenone and Sacile respectively. Not to forget the *Imaginaires en contexte* events which Eric de Kuyper curated in collaboration with the Cinémathèque royale de Belgique (now renamed Cinematek). In order to make audiences experience early cinema's closeness to 19th century culture, Eric de Kuyper arranged screenings at locations which had strong affinities to the subjects of the films shown there. In addition, Eric de Kuyper uses live music as an important tool to bridge the gap between the films and today's audiences who view them a century after their first releases. The musical accompaniment must not necessarily be limited to contemporary music of the 1910s: for example, as he points out, Dmitri Shostakovich's *Symphony No. 8* of 1943 may well evoke the feelings of terror and death which were exited by the products of a steel plant which is exhaustively portrayed in a long industrial film from the First World War.

Recently, a subject-related event comprising five days of early film programmes and lectures was curated by Madeleine Bernstorff and Mariann Lewinsky in Berlin in September 2010, entitled *Frühe Interventionen: Suffragetten – Extremistinnen der Sichtbarkeit* (Early Interventions: Suffragettes – Extremists of Visibility). When they viewed prints in preparing the retrospective, suffragettes appeared to them as if they were spilling their physical presence out into the screening room and thus encroaching into the audience's space. The curators tried to take into account such observations by way of programmes that called attention to the evocative intensity of the films, primarily to be found in anti-suffragette burlesques.

Vanessa Toulmin's compact report on her many screenings of local films from the Mitchell and Kenyon collection to local audiences after more than hundred years underlines the amazing interest in the past of people's own town which provoked many spontaneous reactions from audiences and made these shows a tremendous success all over England. Film performances sometimes borrowed a special aura from the locations of the screenings when they took place in the same town halls where those local films had been screened more than a century ago.

The 'performative turn' of today's early cinema presentations took place in 2007, when the Cinémathèque de la Ville de Luxembourg started the *Crazy Cinématographe* experiment in a fairground tent. The fairground is a most demanding environment which absolutely requires fighting for the attention of the fairground visitors. The film screenings inside the tent must be preceded by a staged front-show to attract passers-by and lure them into the screening room. During the show inside the tent can be observed the resurrection of the film lecturer who had almost disappeared nearly a century ago (with some exception, i.e. the presentations of the Méliès family who still arrange live performances of some of the pioneer's fantastic films).

While almost all live performances of early cinema today which are known to us neglect the historical institution of the film lecturer and instead are satisfied with the musical accompaniment by a piano player or a small orchestra, it is impossible to perform a fairground film show without barkers and film lecturers. Both are absolutely required by the fairground *dispositif* which fundamentally differs from all parameters of film screenings in the environment of film archives and cinema museums. Claude Bertemes and Nicole Dahlen present their remarkable reflections on how they programme the *Crazy Cinématographe* modules in order to defeat the noisy environment at the fairground. They also provide the *Crazy Cinématographe* programme documentation and the *Crazy Cinématographe* filmography which lists every single film shown in the first four years of this experiment's existence.

These contributions written by professional film curators are rounded off with two articles which provide historical and categorical considerations for the comprehension of the different approaches of today's programming and performing early cinema: Andrea Haller and Martin Loiperdinger give a short introduction into the practice of short film programming before the First World War as can be studied in programme advertisements of a German cinema entrepreneur, Peter Marzen, from Trier. Frank Kessler, in his concluding essay, unfolds a wide range of strategies and *dispositifs* which make 'early cinema re-loaded' a varied experience, but always a unique one.

Curating short film programmes of early cinema today sounds somehow similar to curating exhibitions of paintings: programmers try to put the films into an effective running order while aiming at underlining certain aspects of the images projected onto the screen. Every film within a programme stands in a relationship with its previous or following films, which requires much expertise to make the succession of films work as a programme. Given all the differences which might be observed with today's audiences and audiences of a century ago alike, they also have something in common. Now and then, early cinema presented a novelty, a technological one at the turn of the century, an aesthetic one in recent years – so there has always been the element of *surprise* for audiences who watch(ed) early cinema film programmes.

Some contributions in this volume go back to the workshop 'The Art of Programming Early Cinema, Now and Then' which I organised for the Cinémathèque de la Ville de Luxembourg, in September, 2009. Some contributions were written especially for this volume. I feel very grateful to all contributors for their inspiring cooperation.

This volume was made possible through the generous support of the Deutsche Forschungsgemeinschaft (German Research Foundation, DFG) of the Cinémathèque de la Ville de Luxembourg.

Trier, June 2011
Martin Loiperdinger

PART I

Programming and Performing Early Cinema Today – Outstanding Examples

Andrea Haller and Martin Loiperdinger

Stimulating the Audience: Early Cinema's Short Film Programme Format 1906 to 1912

Early cinema reached its widest scope with the commencing boom of fixed-site cinemas from 1906 onward. The large majority of films from the period of early cinema shown again today date from 1906 to 1912. Under the leadership of Pathé, the film producers of that time provided the quickly growing market of fixed-site cinemas with numerous short films of different genres every week. Film distributors and cinema owners collected widely varied programmes from this plentiful offer. Film production expanded: The number of films produced increased, as did the number of copies per film title. Thus, from 1906 to 1912, substantially more films have been preserved than from the preceding years. With the rising output of films, the producers also developed a broader diversity accompanied by intensified standardisation within the genres themselves. Both tendencies met the need to assemble short film programmes following a model of lively alternation. This permitted the cinema owners to offer the audience good entertainment with seven or eight or even up to 20 short films. The 'number' programme of the fixed-site cinemas lasted at least one hour and up to much over two hours. These programmes were changed once or twice, sometimes even three times a week.

Thanks to the efforts employed by film archives throughout the world toward restoration and preservation, we have today again access to the genre diversity of early cinema – and it is easy to recognise the genre the individual films belong to: altogether good prerequisites for designing attractive programmes to familiarise today's audience with early cinema.

This article presents short film programmes from the first years of fixed-site cinema exhibition in Germany. Generally speaking, short film programming was done much the same in most countries of Europe. The programme format was already fixed by 1906: Where did it originate?

Facing page: Front of Marzen's Central-Theater, Trier, 1909, also showing the billboard of Marzen's travelling town hall cinema which was called Edison's Elektrisches Theater.

In his reminiscences of the early days, Colonel Alfred Bromhead, general manager of Gaumont in Britain, tells us that three dominant types of film exhibitors existed before 1906: "1. The fairground travelling showman. 2. The town hall showman. 3. The music hall exhibitor."[1] These entrepreneurs created and standardized three distinct forms of film exhibition: (1) The fairground attraction of the cinematograph show of 15 to 20 minutes, performed in a mobile booth or tent within the environment of other tantalizing fairground attractions; (2) the cinematograph show in town halls, a stand-alone attraction of usually two hours, (3) the cinematograph 'number' of 10 to 15 minutes in music-halls and variety theatres embedded into a programme of live acts.

The fixed-site cinemas established the cinematograph show as a permanent stand-alone entertainment institution. It is the very differences in the duration of the film programmes offered before 1906 which suggest that the fixed-site cinemas reverted to the programming standards of the travelling town hall showmen. In contrast to the travelling fairground showmen, these town hall showmen have seen little research. For example, up to now, only one town hall showman enterprise has been researched for Germany, namely, Marzen's *Edison's Elektrisches Theater* in Trier, which catered to some southwestern regions of Germany: to Lorraine, the Western Palatinate, the Rhineland, and to Luxemburg.[2] For England, case studies exist on several travelling town hall showman enterprises, such as the Thomas-Edison Animated Photo Co., Ralph Pringle's North American Animated Photo Company and Sidney Carter's and Waller Jeffs' New Century Pictures.[3] Some travelling showmen from these enterprises performed stand-alone shows over several months in the same city even before 1906. This means that they had operated already much like a permanent fixed-site cinema, although not throughout the entire year.[4] Enough evidence is now available to evaluate the impact of travelling town hall showman enterprises on the transition to the standards of long and self-sustaining short film programmes, which the rapidly growing number of fixed-site cinemas offered from 1906 onward. In her ground-breaking article on the "cuckoo in the nest" Vanessa Toulmin presents a thorough examination of the three types of film exhibition which dominated the film business before the fixed-site cinema boom.[5] She demonstrates clearly that the stand-alone shows of town hall showmen provided the model for the exhibition practices of fixed-site cinema owners. This conclusion can already be found in her *Electric Edwardians* summarising her research on Mitchell and Kenyon, the film producing company which catered to travelling showmen in the Northwest of England. Vanessa Toulmin states in the chapter on showmanship:

> The lecturer, the use of special effects and the musical accompaniment created a new kind of performance in which the cinematograph was the heart of the exhibition, rather than a mere addition to the music-hall programme or just one of a variety of fairground attractions. The two-hour spectacular promised by the showmen, complete with military band, local films, an effective spieler for the commentary and a change of programme daily, marked the start of a new and

distinct form of leisure activity. Through their business relationship with Mitchell & Kenyon and other companies, the showmen provided a model of how to create a cinema-going habit. By constantly adapting the programme on a daily basis and scheduling the exhibitions for ten- to twelve-week runs in urban centres such as Manchester, Bradford, Liverpool and Birmingham, the stand-alone film exhibitors were anticipating the advent of permanent cinema theatres.[6]

In terms of programming, this was certainly the case when a travelling town hall showman enterprise transformed into a fixed-site cinema entrepreneur as did Marzen's *Edison's Elektrisches Theater*: The Marzen family gave up their renowned travelling town hall shows, and, from March 1909 onward, they operated the Central-Theater in the city centre of Trier.

The short film programme format

The following will take some of the short film programmes of the Central-Theater to discuss profiles of the dramatic lines within the film selection which became typical for the short film programmes of fixed-site cinemas all over Europe between 1906 and 1912. The programme format was rather flexible and allowed a wide variety, depending on numerous factors such as the length of the programme, the place of exhibition, the status of the fixed-site cinema in town, and the profile of the targeted audience in terms of age, gender, race, and class. Altogether, the programme format in European countries remained quite stable until the implementation of long feature films beginning in 1911.

Even a fleeting glance at the design of the playbill clearly indicates that the individual films were not to be considered important in the overall programme composition but that the impression as a whole and the make-up of the entire showing was decisive. The form of the programme was the determining factor, not the content. As something new was to be expected every five to ten minutes, viewers could enter or leave the cinema in the middle of a showing without the fear of having missed anything. This carefree attitude in attending the programme demonstrates that the programme format obeyed certain stand-ards. The viewers at that time had no problems in finding their way into a programme even without knowing just what was being shown, as the pro-gramme followed certain rules and patterns.

Just what such a programme was to look like and what constituted exactly a 'good', i.e. effective and striking, yet wholly tasteful programme – even the cinema owners were not always in agreement. In 1910, the trade journal *Lichtbild-Bühne* established, for example, the following "normal formula", on which the cinema owners were to orient their programmes: "1. Musikpièce, 2. Aktuellität (sic!), 3. Humoristisch, 4. Drama, 5. Komisch, – Pause –, 6. Naturaufnahme, 7. Komisch, 8. Die große Attraktion, 9. Wissenschaftlich, 10. Derbkomisch". ("1. music piece, 2. topical, 3. humorous, 4. drama, 5. comic, – interlude – 6. educational, 7. comic, 8. the great attraction, 9. scientific, 10. coarse comedy").[7] At the end the viewer was to leave the cinema in a good mood.

Central-Theater

Brodstr. 36 — Brodstr. 36

Handelsgerichtlich eingetragene Firma
Inhaber und Besitzer: Peter Marzen.

Programm für Samstag, den 20. August.

Fischerleben. Wunderbare Naturaufnahme.

Der improvisierte Diener. Tolle Humoreske.

Der Traum des Professors Flügel.
Sehr amüsant.

Unter dem Donner der Geschütze.
Packendes Lebensbild. Aeußerst spannend.

Lottchen ist unverbesserlich.
Wahre Lachsalven werden durch die tolle Komik hervorgerufen.

Der treue Hund.
Dieses Bild zeigt uns, wie ein junges Mädchen, von Banditen
überfallen und fortgeschleppt, durch ihren treuen Hund gerettet wird.

Pieske spielt Hausherr.
Pieske hat sich eine neue Wohnung gemietet und fängt an,
dieselbe in Ordnung zu bringen. Aber wie?

„Du sollst nicht".
Ein nachahmenswertes Beispiel der Selbstaufopferung zum
Wohle unserer Nachkommen. Ein Zugstück des Programms.

Riesenbrand der Weltausstellung Brüssel.

Advertisement of the Central-Theater, *Trierischer Volksfreund* (20 August 1910)

The programme of the Trier Central-Theater usually followed a similar model of composition. Marzen's short film entertainment which was advertised in the local newspaper *Trierischer Volksfreund* on 20 August 1911 consisted of nine 'numbers' beginning with FISCHERLEBEN (*Fisherman's life*), presumably a peaceful, idyllic tableau filmed on location. That was followed by a humoresque, DER IMPROVISIERTE DIENER (*The improvised servant*), followed by DER TRAUM DES PROFESSOR FLÜGEL (*Professor Flügel's Dream*) which was announced as "very amusing". The next film, a drama, UNTER DEM DONNER DER GESCHÜTZE (*Under the thunder of guns*), was labelled an "absorbing image of life" and "extremely thrilling". Then came another comedy, LOTTCHEN IST UNVERBESSERLICH (*Lottchen is hopeless*), followed by yet another drama. DER TREUE HUND (*The trusty dog*) presents a young girl attacked by bandits who is saved by her trusty dog. The tension was then relieved by the farce PIEFKE SPIELT HAUSHERR (*Piefke plays master of the house*), only to then lead into the 'box office draw' with the title DU SOLLST NICHT (D.W. Griffith's drama THOU SHALT NOT). The programme finale took up a current subject, the fire at the World's Fair in Brussels.

Stimulating the audience

Guidebooks such as the *Handbuch der praktischen Kinematographie* (Handbook of practical cinematography) by F. Paul Liesegang also offered tips to cinema owners on how to design their showings and programmes to obtain the greatest possible effect. Liesegang emphasised especially the significance of the programme's well thought-out dramatic effect, which was the guarantee for the success of the exhibition, not the individual films.

> The images may be as lovely as they can be, but if they are haphazardly thrown together, their effect can be destroyed; the exhibition's impression as a whole will then in no way turn out to be satisfactory.[8]

He did not consider the films to be autonomous units but as a part of a harmonic whole. Therefore contrasts were to be employed, yet hard contrasts avoided. "It would be a mistake to show frightful tragedy on the heels of a 'knee-slapping comedy'."[9] The mental and emotional contrast of the films was surely to be fraught with tension but was not to be too sharp or without transition. According to Liesegang, the principle of intensification was to be considered. The best film should not be offered as the first 'number', rather a certain intensification should occur to keep "the audience on the edge of their seats".[10] Nor would it be fitting to assemble a programme of only 'hits', which would finally tire and bore the audience.

Accordingly, too much 'attraction' would undermine the entertainment value, just as did repetition and uniformity. Instead, various stimuli for the senses were to be offered using the principles of contrast, intensification, downshifting and a wave-like, rhythmic dramatic effect, as was a diversity of genres and film types.

11

Handelsgerichtlich eingetragene Firma
Alleiniger Besitzer: Peter Marzen.

Die Georgine (Dahlia)
Stereoscopische Blumenstudie. Herrlich koloriert.

Die Frau des Sepoy
Eine wahre Begebenheit aus den Aufständen in Britisch-Indien.

Unsere Lieblinge
Komisches Hundepotpourri in 20 Bildern.
Großer Lacherfolg.

Um die Mutter zu retten
Ergreifendes Drama.

Stierkämpfe in Nimes
Sehr interessante Naturaufnahme.

Onkel Nulpe geht mit seinem Neffen spazieren.
Drollige Burleske.

Paganini
Eine Episode des berühmten französischen Virtuosen Nicolo
Paganini, dem Komponisten der bekannten Variationen des
„Karneval von Venedig."

Max Verfehlt eine reiche Heirat
Komische Szene gespielt von Herrn Max Linder.

Advertisement of the Central-Theater, *Trierischer Volksfreund* (16 January 1911).

The important point, however, was not primarily the mix of genres, i.e. fiction or non-fiction, cartoons or sound-on-disk films (so-called 'Tonbilder') or colour films, topical films or short fiction films, but rather a mixture as diverse as possible of aesthetically effective features and different moods. The programmer was to consider what made up the specific charm of the films, which singular visual appeal they displayed and how they affected the audience: visual pleasure, to be found in both colour films as well as in exotic subjects; the awakening of various emotions, be they sympathy (e.g. in melodramas), suspense (in sensational films but also in so-called 'phantom rides'); or satisfaction of curiosity (moving pictures from distant lands but also sordid dramas). Thus two films of the same genre could follow each other as long as they offered different visual stimuli.

The programme of the Central-Theater advertised on 16 January 1911 presented numerous visual stimuli as well as gratification for the audience. Each film had its own special generic qualities. The first film, DIE GEORGINE (*The dahlia*) charmed the audience with its wonderful colours and its stereoscopic-like images. It was a purely visual attraction and an aesthetic pleasure. The next film, DIE FRAU DES SEPOY (*The Sepoy's Wife*), offered a poignant drama on uprisings in India which transferred the audience to a foreign country and appealed to their sense of empathy. UNSERE LIEBLINGE (*Our darlings*) was a "comical potpourri of dogs" which, besides "getting a big laugh from the audience", provided a bit of an emotional touch at the sight of the cute dogs. The following poignant drama, UM DIE MUTTER ZU RETTEN (*To save the mother*), aroused strong feelings and surely prompted some thought; whereas STIERKÄMPFE IN NÎMES (*Bull fights in Nîmes*) promised something "interesting" and awakened the audience's curiosity about the foreign and extraordinary, perhaps evoking astonishment, excitement or even disgust. This moving picture would have had great visual stimulus, as the viewer was able to see an exotic world, one unknown to the viewer. The droll burlesque ONKEL NULPE GEHT MIT SEINEN NEFFEN SPAZIEREN (*Uncle Nulpe takes a walk with his nephews*) was to evoke laughter and surely provoked malicious glee. A touch of high-brow culture came with the next picture, which narrated an episode from the life of the violin virtuoso Niccolò Paganini and thus contributed to the edification of the audience. The final film, with Max Linder, whom the audience could appreciate as an already known screen personality, then dismissed the audience in a good mood. The viewers had enjoyed aesthetic images, had benefitted from a little education, had gained insights into foreign lands and customs, had experienced excitement and had laughed mightily a few times.

It could even be said that, in a certain manner, not only the films but also the audience was programmed.[11] The programmers undertook not only a time based organisation of various film genres and types of presentation but also an "arrangement of emotions".[12] The programme can thus be understood as a quasi-mechanical experiment to arouse alternating emotional swings and

Central-Theater
Brodstr 36 Brodstr 36

Handelsgerichtlich eingetragene Firma
Alleiniger Besitzer: Peter Marten.

Die letzten Vorgänge in London.

Anarchistenschlacht in Houndsditch.

Schottische Garde im Gefecht. Beschießung der Anarchisten durch
Militär und Polizei von einem gegenüberliegenden Hause.

Fang junger Eisbären in den nördlichen Polargegenden.

Interessante Aufnahme.

Die falsche Anklage.

Dramatische Handlung aus dem modernen Leben.

Furcht vor Einbrechern.

Komische Szene.

Die schwarze Sklavin.

Drama in 10 Abteilungen. Original-Aufnahme aus dem In-
neren Afrikas.

Eine Expreßheirat.

Drollige Humoreske.

Autodafe.

Hochdramatisches Kulturbild aus dem finstersten Mittelalter.
Der spröde Stoff ist in diesem Bilde so meisterhaft behandelt,
alles irgendwie Bedenkliche so rigoros vermieden, daß die Be-
sichtigung desselben ein ästhetischer Genuß ist und eine nachhal-
tige Wirkung auslöst.

Die Elektrisiermaschine.

Sehr amüsant.

Das Waisenkind.

Tragische Szene aus dem Familienleben.
In 14 Abteilungen.

Advertisement of the Central-Theater, *Trierischer Volksfreund* (18 January 1911).

14

moods in the audience through a simple yet extremely effective stimulus-response schema. For example, the composition of the programme observed not only the juxtaposition of different film genres and classifications such as fiction, non-fiction, comedy or fantasy etc. but also the emotional content of the images seen on the screen. The individual films were classified and combined according to their significance for the mood of the audience and the feelings aroused by them and the impact on the viewers' consciousness as well as on their subsequent activities. As Jens Eder suggests, emotions deriving from content can be differentiated from those deriving from aesthetic qualities of the artefact.[13] The former refer to the narration (e.g. the emotion aroused by the sacrificing mother's care for her sick child), the latter to the manner of the presentation (e.g. amazement at visual effects such as running water or speedy camera work in 'phantom rides'). The viewer knew what was to be expected owing to the predictability of the programme sequence in which every film 'number' and the related emotional impulse occupied a certain place or by reading the playbill which normally not only indicated the film type but also the emotional response attached to it ('dramatic', 'knee-slapping funny' etc). The audience could assume with great certainty that, following an emotionally moving film (one making the viewer 'sad' or 'moved'), a different kind of film was programmed to release the emotional tension (i.e. a 'cheerful' piece such as a comedy or an 'untroubled' film such as a travelogue). It was insignificant whether these responses occurred through a film of the same or a different genre. The audience expected and enjoyed this emotional stimulation, enjoyed it especially because such diverse emotional stimuli were offered so densely packed in such a brief time.

> I bought a pack cigarettes, bought a ticket at the box office and was given a playbill which said my ticket was my fare through eastern India and was valid for a trip through Chicago with the tram. On the way, according to the playbill, I was to be deeply moved and would laugh myself silly at various times.[14]

According to this contemporary description, visitors to the cinema began a regular rollercoaster ride of emotions on which the constant ups and downs of such emotions represented the attraction of the journey and/or the programme.

The programme of the Trier Central-Theater advertised on 18 January 1911 demonstrates which emotions the audience was exposed to in viewing a 'number' programme. The opening film of the programme, the contemporary ANARCHISTENSCHLACHT IN HOUNDSDITCH (*Anarchist battle in Houndsditch*), which depicted the siege and shelling of the Latvian revolutionaries who had robbed a jeweller, took the audience to a highly emotional level of excitement right at the start by offering a look at a current incident and permitted them to take part directly in world events. This topical satisfied the audience's desire for sensation. The following FANG JUNGER EISBÄREN IN DEN NÖRDLICHEN POLARGEGENDEN (*Catching young polar bears in the northern polar regions*) as well met the audience's need for sensationalism; they were kept at a highly emotional level of tension. But this travelogue also aroused sympathy, a feeling of solicitude and empathy taking the viewer directly into the next film, the drama

DIE FALSCHE ANKLAGE (*The false accusation*). The emotional tension, held throughout three films, was broken by the following "comical scene", FURCHT VOR EINBRECHERN (*Fear of burglars*) with its comic relief. The audience could laugh heartily and dispel the internal tension. They had hardly recovered somewhat when the next longer drama, DIE SCHWARZE SKLAVIN (*The black slave girl*), promised to offer "original images from the interior of Africa", which doubtlessly spoke to the audience's emotionality on several levels. On the one hand, it again appealed very likely to the viewer's sense of empathy; yet, on the other hand, it satisfied the curiosity about unknown worlds and foreign people and may have sent a (pleasant) shiver through the one or the other. The "droll humoresque" THE EXPRESSHEIRAT (*The speedy marriage*) permitted a breather. The next film, AUTODAFÉ (*Auto-da-fé*), was described as "a highly dramatic *Kulturbild* (image of culture) of the gloomy Middle Ages". AUTODAFÉ portrayed the execution of a judgement by the Inquisition, the guarantee for a shudder. So that fright and dread did not get out of hand, the advertisement had already assured viewers that everything "in any way questionable has been carefully avoided". Thus, according to the advertisement, this sensation-seeking representation of violence was turned into an "aesthetic enjoyment". Next followed THE ELECTRISIERMASCHINE (*The electrifying machine*) an amusing sketch which made the viewers laugh at the antics of the electrified actors. The closing film again exacted a highly emotional response from the audience: the drama DAS WAISENKIND (*The orphan*), a "tragic scene from family life", most probably produced a few tears of pity.

This programme exposed the audience to a continual interplay of tension, sympathy and laughter in which the viewers were constantly kept at a highly emotional level of excitement. The programme advert from the Central-Theater of 18 January 1911 indicates a purely sensational programme exercising emotional demands on the audience. Other programmes in contrast inserted travelogues or other restful images to offer the viewer an emotional break.

Harmful entertainment versus successful business model

The diversity of the short film programme was supported further by the extra-cinematic and performance factors of the film show. Live music accompanied the films; a lecturer led the audience through the programme; projected slides animated the audience to purchase food and drink or requested that viewers remove over-sized hats. These non-cinematic elements made the programme, at least partially, a live event with a great amount of participation and action on the part of the audience. It might be said somewhat exaggeratedly that the audience was a medium in the strictest sense of the word as the final programme was, after all, realised only through the audience sitting in the cinema and their ways of appropriating the programme.

However, there was some criticism of this kind of performance design. Especially conservative intellectuals and the Wilhelminian middle class viewed this kind of seemingly low-brow and sensational entertainment with mistrust.

They criticised primarily that it was not based on contemplation and immersion into the art work; it would speak rather to the lower instincts more or less in a stimulus-response pattern:

> The activating stimulus is as simple as the knee-jerk craving: crime stories with a dozen dead bodies, one gruesome criminal chase after the other; then whopping sentimentality: the dying blind beggar and the dog that croaks on his master's grave; a film with the title: ACHTET DIE ARMEN (*Respect the poor*) or KRABBENFÄNGERIN (*Woman catching crabs*); war ships; no patriotism when they see the Emperor and the army; spiteful shudder.[15]

In fact, this kind of programme design was considered not only unedifying but also harmful, in the physical as well as the psychological sense. The haste and diversity of the programme would overwhelm viewers, would overstimulate their nerves, led to a mental overload and heightening of fantasy and ultimately even to physical impairment. In an essay titled "On the harmful power of suggestion of cinematographic showings", the physician and cinema reformer Albert Hellwig described the alarming reactions of women and children after a cinema showing, ranging from fainting spells to hallucinations to hysteria.[16] The concern for the physical well-being of the cinema audience was, however, always accompanied by the concern for the ethical and moral state of the audience.

On the one hand, one of the strong points of the short film programme lay in this very attentive concern for the audience. The trade press as well as diverse manuals provided the cinema owners with tips on how to set up a showing and its programme in respect to the composition of the audience to achieve the greatest effect possible.

In his *Handbuch der praktischen Kinematographie* (Handbook of practical cinematography), F. Paul Liesegang points to the link between audience and programme design and to the significance of the socio-demographic milieu of the cinema:

> In an industrial city, for example, where there are mostly factory workers, the programme make-up should be different from the one for a rural town or a military base; and then again a different programme for children from that for adults.[17]

The design of the programme was a proven means to stand out from the competitors. As the frequently large-format advertisements in the daily press clearly indicate, the competition among local rivals was also fought out by means of the programme. The mere number of films played a role as much as the musical accompaniment. If the one cinema showed ten films, the other offered a 'first-class gigantic programme' of twelve films the following week. As a result, around 1910, a perceivable tendency emerged to so-called gigantic programmes of more than two hours. And the cinemas did not spare any superlatives to extol their programmes.

The performance of live presentations also served to increase the appeal and audience loyalty. Peter Marzen, cinema owner in Trier, for example, also functioned as film lecturer: As his special highlight, he accompanied the films

Telegramm!

Marzens Edison Theater,
Brodstr. 36.
Unfere eigenen Aufnahmen
I.
Frühjahrsspritzenprobe
unserer freiwilligen Feuerwehr
am 3. Mai am Stadttheater.
II.
Leben und Treiben auf dem
Viehmarkt am 5. Mai. Be-
kannte Trierer Handels-Typen
im Wirken.

Die Aufnahmen find großartig ge-
lungen und werden in jeder Vorstel-
lung vorgeführt. Diese Woche keine
10 sondern 12 Nummern.
Ohne Konkurrenz am Plaße.
Keine alten Vorführungen
Keine Wiederholungen.
Nur erste Neuheiten.

Kommet! Sehet! Staunet!
Die Direktion Wendel Marzen
Telefonruf 1902.

Advertisement of Marzen's Edison Theater, *Trierischer Volksfreund* (15 May 1909).

with commentary in the local dialect.[18] So-called local views offered a further unique feature in reference to the local aspects. In contrast to the usual cinematographic sight-seeing views of cities and towns, these short films were mostly filmed by the cinema owner or commissioned especially for his cinema and were determined for the local audience and did not go into film distribution. They showed primarily important local events such as parades, processions or scenes from city life, i.e. occasions when a great number of townspeople gathered who would later be seen in the film.[19] The viewer was able to discover not only his or her friends and relatives on the screen as well as known places but also, with a bit of luck, him- or herself. The tendency toward permitting the audience to become the producer of 'his/her' pro-gramme becomes clearly apparent particularly in the local views.

Just how popular local views were with the audience can be seen in Marzen's "Telegramm!" advertisement of 15 May 1909 which did not announce the

LEBEN UND TREIBEN AUF DEM VIEHMARKT AM 5. MAI.

entire programme but rather only two local views: FRÜHJAHRSSPRITZENPROBE UNSERER FREIWILLIGEN FEUERWEHR AM 3. MAI AM STADTTHEATER (*Spring hosing practice by our voluntary fire department on 3 May at the City Theatre*) and LEBEN UND TREIBEN AUF DEM VIEHMARKT AM 5. MAI. BEKANNTE TRIERER HANDELS-TYPEN IM WIRKEN (*Life and goings-on at the livestock market on 5 May. Well-known Trier dealer types in action*).

Around 1911, a thorough-going transformation occurred in the film business, one which was mostly noticeable in a rapid change of film programmes. At this time, multiple-reel films entered the market, and 'length', i.e. the duration of the film became the most important criterion. Long feature films were distributed in the exclusive system as singles. They were inserted as a drawing card into the programme and soon began to dominate the programme. Besides these long narrative films the programme continued to embrace five to seven short films of all genres. The focus of the programme shifted to a long feature film, the so-called 'one-hour film'. These films influenced the make-up of the programme and were promoted as the main attraction in the programme advertisements, but they continued to be accompanied and flanked by short films. At the end of 1916, the *Kinematograph* reported,

> Earlier, the programme schedule of a cinema normally showed 8 to 10 different films, sometimes even more. In recent years the focus of the schedule has shifted more and more in favour of the *Schlagerfilm* (hit); today, the most important item in the programme is this long film.[20]

And, in the 1920s, the feature-length motion picture lasting one-and-a-half to two or more hours became the dominating factor for a cinema programme as we are accustomed to it today. In Germany, the principle of variety was preserved with the accompanying programme, consisting of the newsreel and a short comic first feature or a *Kulturfilm*, even into the 1960s.

Translated from German by Frankie Kann

Notes

1. "Proceedings of the British Kinemaograph Society" 21.4 (1933), quoted from John Barnes, *The Beginnings of the Cinema in England 1894–1901*, vol. 4 (1899). Exeter: Exeter University Press, 1996, 77.

2. For a focus on the Marzen family's local films, see Brigitte Braun, Uli Jung, "Local Films from Trier, Luxembourg and Metz: A Successful Business Venture of the Marzen Family, Cinema Owners," *Film History* 17 (2005): 19–28. See also Uli Jung, "Travelling Cinematograph Shows in the Greater Region of Luxembourg. An Overview" in Martin Loiperdinger (ed.), *Travelling Cinema in Europe. Sources and Perspectives* (Frankfurt am Main/Basel: Stroemfeld, 2008), 93–101; Paul Lesch, "Travelling Cinematograph Shows in Luxembourg", ibid., 103–117; Brigitte Braun, "Marzen's Travelling Town Hall Cinematograph in the Greater Region of Luxembourg", ibid., 119–126.

3. Vanessa Toulmin, "The Importance of the Programme in Early Film Presentation", *KINtop* 11 (2002): 19–33; Jon Burrows, "Waller Jeffs' Scrapbooks", *Picture House: Journal of the Cinema Theatre Association* 29 (2004): 44–55; Vanessa Toulmin, "'We take them and make them': Mitchell and Kenyon and the Travelling Exhibition Showmen" in Vanessa Toulmin, Simon Popple and Patrick Russell (eds), *The Lost World of Mitchell and Kenyon. Edwardian Britain on Film* (London: Bfi Publishing, 2004), 59–68. Richard Brown, "New Century Pictures: Regional Enterprise in Early British Film Exhibition", ibid., 69–82.

4. See recently on T.J. West in Bournemouth: Jon Burrows, "West is Best; or, what we can learn from Bournemouth", *Early Popular Visual Culture* 8 (2010): 351–362.

5. Vanessa Toulmin, "Cuckoo in the Nest: Edwardian Itinerant Exhibition Practices and the Transition to Cinema in the United Kingdom from 1901 to 1906", *The Moving Image* 10.1 (2010), 51–79.

6. Toulmin, *Electric Edwardians*, 74.

7. "Grundregeln für die Programmzusammenstellung", *Lichtbild-Bühne* 3.116 (14 October 1910).

8. Paul F. Liesegang (ed.), *Handbuch der praktischen Kinematographie* (Leipzig: Liesegang Verlag, 1908), 231.

9. Ibid.

10. Ibid.

11. François Jost, "Die Programmierung des Zuschauers", *KINtop* 11 (2002): 35–47.

12. Frank Kessler, Sabine Lenk and Martin Loiperdinger (eds), "Editorial", *KINtop* 11 (2002): 7. See also Jens Eder, "Vom Wechselbad der Gefühle zum Strom der Stimmungen. Affektive Aspekte des Programms" in Ludwig Fischer (ed.), *Programm und Programmatik. Kultur- und medienwissenschaftliche Analysen* (Constance: UVK, 2005), 371–385.

13. Eder, 375.

14. Gustav Melcher, "Von der lebenden Photographie und dem Kino-Drama", *Der Kinematograph* 112 (17 February 1909).

15. Alfred Döblin, "Das Theater der kleinen Leute", *Das Theater* 1.8 (December 1909); quoted from Jörg Schweinitz (ed.), *Prolog vor dem Film. Nachdenken über ein neues Medium 1909-1914* (Leipzig: Reclam, 1992), 155.

16. Albert Hellwig, "Über die schädliche Suggestionskraft kinematographischer Vorführungen", *Ärztliche Sachverständigen-Zeitung* 20.6 (15 March 1914): 119–124.

17. Liesegang, *Handbuch*, 231.

18. Cf. Martin Loiperdinger, "'The Audience Feels rather at Home ...' Peter Marzen's 'Localisation' of Film Exhibition in Trier" in Frank Kessler and Nanna Verhoeff (eds), *Networks of Entertainment. Early Film Distribution 1895–1915* (Eastleigh: John Libbey, 2007), 123–130.

19. See Uli Jung, "Local Views: a blind spot in the historiography of Early German Cinema", *Historical Journal of Film, Radio and Television* 22.3 (2002): 253–273. A contemporary article from the local newspaper *Trierische Zeitung* offers an amusing report about the cinema owner and lecturer Peter Marzen and his film lectures in Trier dialect and about the special attraction of the local views he presented: "Ein 'trierischer' Kinematograph 1909", reprinted in *KINtop* 9 (1999): 11–13.

20. Walter Thielemann, "Programmwechsel unserer Lichtspielbühnen", *Der Kinematograph* 10.518 (29 November 1916).

PART I

Programming and Performing Early Cinema Today – Outstanding Examples

Mariann Lewinsky

The Best Years of Film History:
A Hundred Years Ago

for Chiara Caranti

In the summer of 2003 the festival Il Cinema Ritrovato presented a series of five programmes of films from 1903, curated and introduced by Tom Gunning. I do not know how this came about. The section was called, in English, *The First Great Year of Cinema: 1903* and, in Italian, *Cento anni fa: I film del 1903*.

My involvement dates from April 2004, when the director of the Cineteca di Bologna, standing beside me, was wondering to himself whether the *Hundred Years Ago* series should continue and, if so, who might curate it that year – and muttering that it was, in any case, now too late as the festival starts at the end of June. I muttered back to him that I could do it – a remark which has afforded me the happiest seven years of my career.[1]

It is mostly thanks to the films. The body of work produced from 1904 to 1910 is the most interesting in the whole of cinema history, for it was then, as it would never be again, that a whole host of aesthetic and narrative possibilities of the medium were explored and tested. It is also the least known and most undervalued work. Moreover, films of this period have to be properly programmed, for screenings to be a success. All this makes the curator's job both challenging and rewarding. We are talking about films or fragments with running times of between one minute and fifteen (except for the exceptions, of course). Choosing between hundreds of short films, grouping the chosen titles into programmes and putting them into an effective running order, with films being dropped or exchanged the whole time, is a job which can be done well or badly. It is as important to the way the films are received as the staging of a play is to its success. I aim, via my programming, to make the selected films accessible and to provide a context for them by the way they are combined, so

Facing page: Rediscovered by *A Hundred Years Ago*: Mistinguett was not only a famous star of the revue theatres in the 1920, but also a great actress in Pathé films from 1908 onward.
Film poster from the Collection Fondation Jérôme Seydoux-Pathé.

that each film's special qualities are shown to their best advantage and each film's position in the programme fulfils a dramatic function. A badly-constructed programme reduces or destroys the audience's ability to see, think and feel. But we have arrived far too quickly at these reflections on programming principles. So let us return to these rarely-seen films of before 1910.

Films before 1910 (or 1920) in non-specialist and in specialist circles

What is one dealing with? An amorphous, confusing mass of thousands of totally unknown film titles and as many names which also mean nothing to most people. Gaston Velle? Albert Capellani? Renée Carl? Raymond Frau? There are no landmarks. How to find a way through? What to look for? What might be interesting and what unimportant? And is there an audience for these stone age works, or will five people turn up for an evening which has cost enormous amounts of time, nervous wear and tear and money to organise?

It is understandable that people who might programme films from before 1910 (or 1914 or 1920), people managing film societies or festivals without this specialised focus, tend to steer clear. And so it is that the situation persists: in books, in the programmes of municipal cinemas and even (it does still happen) in university courses, the first 25 years of cinema history are no more than a curtain-raiser to the 'real thing'. Dealing with them seems a tiresome duty, with the obligatory 'Pioneers' chapter (Lumière-Méliès-Griffith) and at best one more specimen from the 1910s (either an Asta Nielsen film, an Italian historical spectacular or INTOLERANCE). Cinema history de facto is considered to start properly in 1920, when we get under way with the great comic actors and classics of the silent film: there are Flaherty and Dreyer, Murnau and Eisenstein, Lubitsch and Garbo, Metropolis and Napoleon. Whatever came before 1920 remains unknown and is not shown or talked about, even to audiences and readers who are, in principle, interested, cultured cinephiles. Only Verdi, never Handel, only steak, never oysters. To acquire an 'acquired taste' you need time and opportunity.

In the world of specialised research and film archives, on the other hand, the pre-1920 cinema has gained in stature over recent decades. It has grown into a respected area of research, is conserved and restored. This higher status also finds expression in a change in terminology: nobody these days talks about "primitive" film (which was once the standard term).[2] At the Brighton conference of FIAF in 1978, which marked the beginning of this new interest on the part of archivists and film historians, films from the first decade of cinema (1900 to 1906) were shown, though at that stage non-fiction film was excluded. Our astonishment now at this idea – for how can you study Italian cookery if you exclude pasta? – is a measure of how much more knowledgeable we are these days. For this we have the many researchers to thank (and the creation in 1985 of Domitor, the society for the study of early cinema), their publications (such as the *KINtop* yearbook for early film, 1992–2006), international

Hundreds of films were viewed for *A Hundred Years Ago* and then screened in Bologne. Numerous films were identified and restored as for example Albert Capellani's L'ARLÉSIENNE (France 1908). Front of the Alhambra cinema in Rochefort-sur-Mer. Picture postcard from the Collection Fondation Jérôme Seydoux-Pathé.

archive projects (such as the Projeto Lumière and the Search for Lost Films, 1991–1996) as well as – and especially – the annual festivals Le Giornate del Cinema Muto in Pordenone (since 1981) and Il Cinema Ritrovato in Bologna (since 1986).

Collecting experiences, taking a position

Two experiences which were particularly important to me were the first two workshops of the Nederlands Filmmuseum (NFM, now known as EYE – Film Institute Netherlands), *Non-fiction from the 1910s* (1994) and *Disorderly Order – Colours in Silent Film* (1995). For three days we viewed films and had open discussions in a group of about fifty specialists, archivists, film historians and filmmakers. The film programmes, devised by the curators of the NFM, were brilliantly conceived, with new experimental films also included. We sat for hours in front of that screen, watching tirelessly in excited anticipation, picture by picture, insatiable.[3] Some of the films I encountered for the first time there are now among my favourites: beautiful, astonishing works such as LES GRANDES EAUX DE VERSAILLES, THE DAINEF SISTERS, LITTLE TICH, THE DYTISCUS and CHILDREN'S REFORMATORY.[4] "A life is incomplete, if one has not seen a marmot", as my first employer, Frank Sternberg, once told me. A dealer in ancient coins and emigrant from Berlin (and Rome and the USA and again Germany) he had ended up in Switzerland, and made the comment after an excursion to the Swiss National Park, where he had hoped to see marmots but failed. Well, yes, life is equally incomplete if you have never seen THE

DAINEF SISTERS. Or the frog and the salamander ballet and the delirious play of colours due to nitrate decomposition in LA LÉGENDE DU FANTÔME (1908). Or the pure graphic and kinetic beauty of the scene in LA COURSE DES BELLES-MÈRES (1907), where patterned bundles roll diagonally across the screen (they are men in baggy, flowered dresses, tumbling down a grassy hillside, playing the eponymous mothers-in-law). Or the hardships, the boy's poverty and the magnificent flowering apple trees – are there still such orchards today? – in CHILDREN'S REFORMATORY. Or Linder's charm and perfect body language in LOVER'S ILL LUCK (LES PÉRIPÉTIES D'UN AMANT, 1907), when he was not yet the world-famous Max, "King of Cinematography" (*Pathé Bulletin hebdo-madaire* 1911), but an unnamed player, as all were in those days.

In other words, I pass on to others films I value highly, films that will, I believe, enrich and cheer the lives of their viewers.

The curators of the Amsterdam workshops were clearly inspired by their former artistic director, Eric de Kuyper, a creative genius when it comes to programming difficult material.[5] If, in the pantheon of film archivists, Lindgren and Langlois personify the opposing principles of preserving and exhibiting then, in the programming of short films from before the first World War, de Kuyper represents the understanding of these films as aesthetic events and a determination to bring them to life in a successful show, a performance. At the opposite end of the spectrum is a model of programming which is considered perfectly normal and is to be experienced, or suffered, everywhere: lots of examples of the same thing, neatly sorted, such as all the films of a particular director in chronological order or lots of films with comic actors screened in the alphabetical order of the names of the performers.

What is the point of a practice which is fatal both to films and to audiences? I can understand it, as an effort to make the material accessible to "research" (an abstract, disembodied entity) in as neutral a format as possible. In this setting, the films are to be understood and used as source materials and the systematic presentation is intended to protect the audience from unscientific sensations such as amazement or delight: the event re-enacts not a show at the cinema but a lesson in the classroom, to be drilled in sitting still and remaining attentive while enduring extreme boredom – the legitimacy a priori guaranteed. Or I can judge this approach to be simply the cheapest solution to the problem. The screening of films in chronological or alphabetical order needs no experience and not a moment's thought – not even any preparatory viewing.

To do one thing but not dismiss the other; to entertain the audience but at the same time educate; to understand and present these films in their dual nature, both as documents of a past time but also as an aesthetic experience in the present day: these are whispered promptings from my karma and from literary theoretician Peter Szondi. A film historian with no interest in producing theory, who finds writing an ordeal, found her medium in programming: film historiography by means of the films themselves. Something like the bonsai – for a bonsai pine is both a real, living pine and at the same time an artefact, the

Programming *A Hundred Years Ago* features non-fiction films of the past which mirror the present.
Au Maroc: Tanger (France 1909).

representation of a pine achieved by simplification, miniaturisation and clari-
fication. Dolf Sternberger offers another appropriate description. He called his
Panorama of the 19th Century (1938) an attempt to reveal the topography of the
past by means of quotations. But the quotations do not serve to prove theses:
they are the medium of his attempt to make the past legible, in the characters
and flourishes of its writings. – Meanwhile, I asked Gian Luca Farinelli why
he had initiated the *Hundred Years Ago* series in 2003 and this was his response:
"I felt that early cinema was still not screened or explored sufficiently, even at
the two major festivals, Pordenone and Bologna, so I looked for a formula
which could continue over several years". A great advantage to the format of a
series in which each year's programme is dedicated to a single year's production
is that it precludes the evolutionary approach: the audience sees the films of a

specific historical moment in the correct context, i.e. together with many other films of that moment, and not as forerunners of something (implicitly more developed) which is to come.

Process

But enough of these preliminaries: now we come to the heart of the matter. The process is always the same. I visit film archives, view there all the films they have from the given year, and while I am viewing I make a few notes on each film, by hand. As well as production details (company and, if known, director and actors) and informations about the print (length, colour process, intertitle language, state of completeness and photographic quality) I also note judgements ("lousy print of a good film", "horses hardly stirring – magical") as an aid to selection, as well as key words about the content as an aide-memoire. Sometimes there are also tags (such as 'military' or 'dance'), which make possible thematic kernels around which programmes might form. After visiting an archive, I go through my notes and produce – again by hand – a list of the best. There are always, in addition, a couple of films for which dating or identification is missing, insufficient or incorrect, and these I look into. You can find a lot in Birett and Bousquet.[6] My archive visits are limited to Europe: Paris, London and Amsterdam have particularly large collections. I view the films on an editing table or, rarely (in Prague and Amsterdam), I have the luxury of seeing them projected.[7]

The end product is a series of programmes[8] including 'systematic' and 'freestyle' programmes – like the compulsory and free elements in figure skating competitions. Systematic programmes have a monographic subject, such as a production company (Vitagraph 1906, Saturn 1907) or country (Great Britain, USA, Denmark) or a specific holding (1905 films from the Abbé Joye collection, 1906 films from the Goldstaub collection). I usually give these programmes to curators who specialise in the relevant area. Since 2005 Giovanni Lasi has curated the Italian programmes.

A special case of a systematic programme is the reconstruction of a historical programme. It need not be absolutely precise or complete – but the audience should get the opportunity to see from time to time a historically anchored example of a varied programme. A related exercise is the tribute to an event in cinema history, such as our opening programme of 2009, comprising films shown at the first ever film festival, in Milan in 1909, or the partial reconstruction in 2008 of the premiere of L'ASSASSINAT DU DUC DE GUISE, which had taken place on 17 November 1908 in the Salle Charras. Cinema history did not happen in a vacuum and one of the great wonders of cinematography is that, a hundred years ago, it captured photographically pieces of the visible world and we can see these in the present day. For this reason I always work into the programmes some films relating to important events or to contemporary conditions: electricity in 1904, revolt in Odessa and mutiny on the

Rediscovered by *A Hundred Years Ago*. Freedom for women in comedies before the First World War. LEA GIUNCHI IN LEA SI DIVERTE (Italy 1911).

Potemkin in 1905, French and Spanish occupation of Morocco in 1907 and the first Paris season of the Ballets russes in 1909.

The freestyle programmes

The other programmes – about half the series – I put together freestyle. What that means can be gleaned from the festival catalogues: *Spots and Combinations* (2005), *Visions sensuelles* (2008), *A Cinema of Distraction* (2009) and *Landscape and Narrative* (2010). A film series has much in common with an exhibition, and in the programmes, as in glass display cases, I set out what the films have to offer in the way of topics, qualities, idiosyncrasies. I suggest possible access routes which strike me as interesting and conducive to an understanding of the films. To consider these films only as source material for film history is, I think, wrong. "The sun does not shine so that cabbages can grow" (Georg Lichtenberg, circa 1770). It is wrong because it exploits them, and wrong because it loses sight of their main *raison d'être*. Like a fervent pagan, on a mission to save the souls of half-hearted Christians, I pelt my audience with apples from the tree of knowledge and hope to divert them from the path of received wisdom.

During the viewings, the focal points of the freestyle programmes crystallise, possible configurations occur to me, films fall into groups in my head and in my notes. I select: firstly (talent spotting) the most beautiful and the best films and, secondly, (looking for trends), where there is a large-ish group, I choose the representative films that I need in order to give an impression of the genres, subjects, motifs or technical processes popular in a given year. I give myself carte blanche in the selection and am never unsure. Is this a gourmet's flair? Unerringly spotting the juiciest pear in the basket? Like knowing, when tasting bean soup, that it needs a bit more orange peel and then it will be perfect?

I construct the programmes on a big table, using strips of paper with film titles on them, and aiming at the right length and density, for a programme of short films must not be too long or too rich. Guy Borlée books the films and Chiara Caranti, the technical coordinator, puts them together. Before the festival Chiara and I have a trial screening so that we can, if necessary, make last-minute adjustments, e.g. changing a film's position in the running order or dropping it entirely if the programme would work better without it. We also establish the best projection speed for each individual film, agree any further arrangements for the show and so on.

I feel obliged to make a mental note, in the film tally going on in my head, of any biases, any element which is over- or under-represented in the series of a given year. Sometimes this has happened for pragmatic reasons. For example, up to the end of 2008 when the copyrights expired, it was impossible to show Georges Méliès films except under conditions dictated by the rights-holders. Other biases are the product of my personal tastes. Historical costume films were extremely important from 1908 onward. But I prefer films set in antiquity and in the 18th century and tend to avoid those set in the Middle Ages and the Renaissance, in order to show this genre at its best. For costume dramas, which were highly valued in their time, with their intriguing potential for bringing the past to life, are a hundred times harder today for an audience to accept than non-fiction or comic scenes.

At the festival and elsewhere

In the Bologna festival situation I am relieved of the task of finding viewers for these films, which are certainly no audience magnets. A certain proportion of those attending the festival will sit all day in the 'blue auditorium' of the Lumière cinema and watch everything that hits the screen. I do not know what they make of my freestyle programmes. Academics seem to prefer hunting down individual films or individual phenomena, while archivists discern more clearly the configuration of the programmes. Apart from a handful of friends and fans, audiences are reserved, either practised festival attendees or pretending to be. Yet *A Hundred Years Ago* is considered an important section of the festival, has been allocated a good deal more festival time over the years and – witness this article – has now reached a point where I have to talk and write about my programming. So this is my chance to declare publicly that neither the films since 1904 nor the programme series since 2004 have improved. "No progress in pleasures, nothing but mutations" (Roland Barthes), and I regret that – though I could be imagining this – the general positive feedback only seemed to begin after we had already gone past the years up to and including 1907, which are my favourites, the most experimental.

Rediscovered by *A Hundred Years Ago*. Albert Capellani did not only direct masterpieces of the 1910s such as LES MISÉRABLES (France 1912) and GERMINAL (France 1913), but he was since late 1905 one of the most important directors of his times. MARIE STUART (France 1908).

So it was interesting to compare the reactions when, in 2010, at the 56th International Short Film Festival Oberhausen, Eric de Kuyper and I presented, to a festival audience which was knowledgeable and sophisticated but not well versed in the cinema of this period, ten freestyle programmes under the title *From the Deep. The Great Experiment 1898–1918*. Here, the joy and rapt amazement in the screening room were almost palpable. Beaming with pleasure, people would stop us in the street to thank us: they had had an important encounter, like my own fifteen years earlier in Amsterdam.

It is rare that I can present a programme in an ordinary cinema, but it does happen from time to time. Compared with festival-goers in Bologna and Oberhausen, these audiences are free of prejudice and of the compulsion felt by the specialists to turn everything to some professional use. Ordinary viewers talk openly, after a screening, about how hard they have found it at first to 'get into' these unfamiliar works and are always touched by such close encounters with the visible world of the past. And then there are the personal applications: a lady enthusiastic about the table linen and gloves she had noticed; an ancient history expert admiring the accuracy of scenery and costumes in a drama set in that period; and all of them delighted to have laughed so much at Foolshead and the stupid policemen.

I am an ordinary viewer. The magic of these close encounters with the visible past has never waned. There is the feeling of being an unforeseen, even unauthorised spectator and this brings to my relationship with the films an element I cannot entirely fathom. Some kind of positive tension. It is hard to grasp the fact that thousands of these films, produced for their short season a hundred years ago, for five minutes of entertainment, are here with us in our present day and that we are able to watch them. That they once more release their merriment and their beauty. Here are more marmots than a human had a right to expect.

Conclusion

We are watching MES FILLES PORTENT LA JUPE-CULOTTE (Pathé, 1911). The father has just opened the wardrobe: "There's something missing! Aha! My wife and daughters have taken my trousers! But I, dear audience, have a great idea. Now I'm going to pinch a skirt out of their wardrobe!"

The actor playing the father is bubbling over with expressive energy, communicating with the audience. He explains to us his moods and intentions and shows us his new costume. He is an actor and at the same time a narrator. A *benshi* could use my translation into words of the looks and gestures as his libretto.

People who constructed their films like this had in mind the future screening situation. Acknowledging and making use of this, filmmakers of the period created a collaborative relationship between the screen and the audience: "You are watching me, viewer, and I am showing you terrific things!" That is how the comedy scenes work. In documentary scenes no secret is made of the filming process: factory workers have obviously made a special visit to the hairdresser the previous day, and look up from their work, smiling at the camera. In dramatic scenes, there is no pressing the empathy button. Instead, viewers have a free hand in "writing their own soul text".[9]

All this is sometimes taken as a sign that this cinema has not yet totally got the hang of the job and is still rather naïve. In the course of these seven years I have lost any ideas I might have had about naivety in these films. The filmmakers were highly professional. They produced a normal Gaussian bell curve with most films of average quality and belonging to the mainstream, a few sublime achievements at one end and some at the other end utter rubbish. They knew their viewers and treated them very well, and us with them. Who could ask for anything more?

Translated from German by Clare Kitson

Notes

1. The author was curator for the Il Cinema Ritrovato festival, the *Cento anni fa / A Hundred Years Ago* programme series for the years 1904, 1905 and 1907–1911. For 1906 Andrea Meneghelli was the main curator.

2. The Gaumont-Pathé-Archives website still uses "primitive" as a tag. Such qualifications, and also the category of "early" cinema are misleading and unnecessary: a production year or period (from year x to year y) is sufficient.

3. For an extensive report see: Mariann Lewinsky, "Im Museum, in der Akademie, halblaut", in: *Neue Zürcher Zeitung* No. 99 (29/30 April 1995).

4. LES GRANDES EAUX DE VERSAILLES (F 1904, Pathé), LES SIX SŒURS DAINEF (F 1902, Pathé). LITTLE TICH (F 1907, Pathé), LE DYTIQUE (F 1911, Eclair), LE BAGNE DES GOSSES (F 1907, Pathé).

5. Examples for his experimental presentations are *Bits and Pieces*, *Imaginaires en contexte* and *Concerts en images*.

6. Herbert Birett, *Das Filmangebot in Deutschland 1895–1911* (München: Filmbuchverlag Winterberg, 1991); Henri Bousquet, *Catalogue Pathé des années 1896–1914* (4 vols., Bures-sur-Yvette: 1993–1996).

7. It is impossible to assess a film's quality from viewing on DVD or YouTube as in these transfers you will miss textures, proportions, colours, complex images, the play of light – and generally most of what makes a film worth seeing.

8. In 2009 the *Hundred Years Ago* section reached its maximum extent, with twelve programmes. In 2010 we reorganised the section, making the programmes rather longer but there were fewer of them: eight, one each day of the festival.

9. Victor Klemperer made this observation in his wonderful essay "Das Lichtspiel", published 1912, reprinted in Fritz Güttinger (ed.), *Kein Tag ohne Kino. Schriftsteller über den Stummfilm* (Frankfurt am Main: Deutsches Filmmuseum, 1984), 75–85. During a film screening, he writes, the viewers "are at every moment forced and at the same time enabled to create souls for the moving bodies on the screen, or, to put it more simply, to write themselves the narration for the pictures (...) this constant activity of breathing life into the film (...) makes the viewer an active collaborator (...) he is forced to participate in the creation and the emotions" (quoted from Güttinger, 83-84).

Tom Gunning

'From the Bottom of the Sea':
Early Film at the Oberhausen Festival

Man Ray once said: "The worst films I've ever seen, the ones that send me to sleep, contain ten or fifteen marvelous minutes. The best films I've ever seen only contain ten or fifteen valuable minutes." A tee shirt for sale at the 56th International Short Film Festival at Oberhausen puts it even more succinctly, if less elegantly: "Fuck Feature Films". The dominance of the feature length (roughly, an hour plus) form for film has lasted for almost a hundred years and has determined (and been supported by) systems of distribution and funding, and, perhaps even more crucially, has controlled cultural attitudes towards what films do, formally and structurally. Although there are exceptions, the 90 minute to two hour format reinforces film's role as a narrative medium, and its homology to the novel and the three act drama as the major Western form of long format storytelling.

Although forms like television have found niches for shorter formats, short films remain outriders within the commercial industry, whether as scouts, spies, or saboteurs. Short films cost less, and have the maneuverability of guerrilla outfits compared to the full battalion strength feature film, with its armies of support, and vast supply lines of material. Oberhausen supports the short form against all comers, and remains perhaps most famous as the launching site for the revolt against *Papa's Kino* that led to the New German Cinema in the sixties. It still feels different from any other major film festival – younger, less formal, more edgy and its attention to avant-garde and alternative cinemas (both current and retrospective) continues to exist side by side with the potentially more commercial categories of music videos and animation.

But the first lesson revolutionaries must master teaches that every system of dominance has a history and an origin. This year Oberhausen, not without debate and controversy, decided to place the far reaches of that history on display. The feature film may be about a century old, but cinema is older than

---

Facing page: Cover of Festival Catalogue: 56th International Short Film Festival, Oberhausen.

LE BAGNE DES GOSSES (Pathé, 1907).

that, and for approximately its first two decades (until, say, the First World War) the short film form held sway, with few films made that lasted more than fifteen minutes. Although narratives of progress often attribute this brevity to a primitive stage of development or to technical limitations, neither is true. Early short films, rather than being infantile sketches of more sophisticated forms, developed their own logics and structures, their own ways of addressing audiences and their own delights.

Freelance curator and programmer Mariann Lewinsky and Eric de Kuyper (former deputy director of the Netherlands Filmmuseum which has done so much to rediscover early cinema) put together a unique series of 10 programs, each carefully arranged, of approximately one hundred films. The title for this thread of the festival says a great deal: *From the Deep: The Experimental Film 1898-1918*. Programming and even viewing the films demanded an act of excavation, of bringing up something that had been buried. The German title carries an even stronger freight of metaphor: "*Vom Meeresgrund*", from the bottom of the sea (which led one friend of mine to think the programme were dedicated to early underwater photography). The programme lived up to this promise of penetrating into unknown territory where monsters and treasure might lurk. To call these experimental film may seem anachronistic, and it does have a polemical edge. These films often seem avant-garde today, which was not part of their intention, but they *were* experiments: in what the medium could do and what audiences would enjoy. Cinema was discovered in this era;

Les Grandes Eaux de Versailles (Pathé 1904).

it tried out approaches and genres, methods and techniques; it nearly exploded with experimental energy.

This principle formed the keynote of Lewinsky and Kuyper's programming: not to present the early history of cinema or even the evolution of film art, but to rediscover the pure chaos, delight and 'anything can happen' aspect of early cinema, an energy as relevant to the spirit of Oberhausen as it is foreign to much of commercial filmmaking. The plumbing of the depth undertaken by this programme recalls Jules Verne's subterranean adventures more than an academic archeology. Each programme therefore, although often grouped around themes (e.g. colour in early film or images of labor, travel, or the new woman) reflected the delight in variety and sudden juxtapositions that early cinema offered. Comedies jostle with actualities; vaudeville acts follow panoramas of tourist views. I have claimed that an aesthetic of astonishment dominated early cinema. These programs resurrected that sense of surprise at every turn, a greedy and undisciplined camera eye gaping at a new modern world, and seeming to exclaim, "Look here, look there". Voracious in its appetite, untrammeled in its taste for speed and destruction, vulgar, curious and rarely well behaved.

Did it work? In contrast to the film buffs and scholars who show up for the festivals dedicated to silent cinema in Pordenone or Bologna, could these films without stars, often without plots, sometimes incomplete, always unfamiliar, attract a younger audience weaned on music video and avant-garde films? There had been some doubts before the festival, but as soon as the inaugural programme had screened they evaporated. Every programme was packed, usually with the overflow sitting in the aisles, as a new audience discovered these films, realizing that film history did not have to be a simple narrative of progressive mastery of a commercial film language, but rather a youthful exploration of an art that did not yet have any rules or traditions (exactly the basis on which these films were attacked by reformers in all countries in this era). The laughter as audiences discovered a chaos of violent comedy that predated Chaplin; the gasps of appreciation as they viewed the phantasmagoric range of hues that hand coloured films could produce; or the somber recognition of the often horrifying visions a modernizing and imperialist world offered in the brutal treatment of native people and nature – all of these reactions exceeded the preconceptions many people had of what the first decades of cinema offered.

The programmers recognized they were addressing a modern audience, and there was no attempt to 'recreate' a historical picture show. Musical accompaniment by Donald Sosin was wisely supplied (in spite of some opposition) and often gave a witty sense of the freedom pianist practiced in this era, but with little attempt to actually recreate a historical performance. The selection of films certainly tended towards the bizarre and outrageous (but having seen a large proportion of the existing silent films I maintain that this reflects the period, especially before 1912). But while acknowledging the historical distance between audiences at Oberhausen in 2010 and these films, the programmes managed to channel the vibrant fun of early cinema, rather than embalm it through a historical contextualization. Ironically, in doing this it delivered a more accurate sense of film programming than is often offered by museum programs. The programmes deliberately mixed fiction and actuality (or as we tend to call them today, documentary) films. Later cinema tends to separate these film aesthetically and programmatically. Seeing comedies on suffragettes next to newsreel footage of their marches gives a different sense of history than the current recycling of early footage in the pedestrian programmes of the History Channel. Modes of address collided in early cinema, rather co-operated, and these programme deliberately reproduced that. Thus a Pathé stencil coloured fairy film LA PEINE DU TALION from 1906 featuring hourglass waisted dancing girls in butterfly costumes skewering a male entomologist on a cork was followed by an early scientific fly of an acrobatic fly in huge close-up performing a series of weight lifting tricks. A Pathé trick film LE BON INVALIDE ET LES ENFANTS, in which an old man allows kids in a park to use his detachable head as a ball and his arms as a bat, was followed by a slow-motion film of athletes jumping hurdles and climbing ropes. Footage of the Kaiser's family relaxing on a balcony after a state wedding was followed by a dramatic reenactment of the assassination of the Russian Interior Minister Plehvie. These specific juxtapositions were arranged, of course, by the programmers, but they reflect the mix of materials and moods that characterized early film shows.

Transformations in meaning brought on by history were matched by the material transformation that time works on film prints. While the loss of the majority of early film to the decay of nitrate film represents a tragedy that could have been prevented (if foresight and money had been available), nitrate decay nonetheless brings on strange beauties (which form the material of the more recent films DECASIA by Bill Morrison and LYRICAL NITRATE by Peter Delpeut). The programs featured a number of decayed film precisely for their aleatory delights of blurring features and distorted space. Even more crucial to the programming was the principle pioneered by de Kuyper at the Nederlands Museum (and continued by the insightful current archivists there) of preserving little bits of films whose context had disappeared (fragments which many archives would throw away). Gathered into programmes called *Bits and Pieces* (of which about a half an hour were shown in one Oberhausen programme), the fragments not only preserve stray moments of beauty, but carry the sort of enigmatic poetry that modern art and literature have discovered in the fragment, a glimpse of mystery never to be solved. More than any other aspect of this programming, this fascination embodied in piece of which we will never get the whole expresses surprising aesthetic discoveries the archive can offer and that this festival made available to a more general audience.

Will Oberhausen continue to offer such programmes? I hope so. More films wait to be rescued from the archive shelf. The past always has a future – if people make it available in as creative a manner as *From the Deep*.

FRÜHE
INTERVENTIONEN
SUFFRAGETTEN

EXTREMISTINNEN
DER
SICHTBARKEIT

PROGRAMM

23.9. – 27.9.2010

ZEUGHAUSKINO
DEUTSCHES HISTORISCHES
MUSEUM

Madeleine Bernstorff

From the Past to the Future:
Suffragettes – Extremists of Visibility
in Berlin

Feminism is increasingly being declared outdated, a mere museum piece: there is, the argument runs, nothing more to fight for and the agenda of the 1970s is well and truly obsolete.[1] It was against this apparently postfeminist backdrop that a film programme entitled *Frühe Interventionen: Suffragetten – Extremistinnen der Sichtbarkeit* (Early Interventions: Suffragettes – Extremists of Visibility) ran at the Zeughauskino, the cinema of the Deutsches Historisches Museum, Berlin, and met with an overwhelming response.[2] The project was based on the observation that the women's suffrage movement became radicalised at almost exactly the same time as cinema, still in the process of self-invention, began to consolidate itself and to shrug off nineteenth-century forms of expression. This historical conjunction is revealed in numerous newsreels and comedies. My choice of title for the series was intended to show very clearly where my primary interest lay: in the portrayal of rebellion, activism and an often high-spirited intervention against the ruling order at a time when cinema was itself experiencing a radical upheaval. I also wanted to show not only that the films made between 1900 and 1914 generally satirise the movement for emancipation, but also that the movement itself strategically deployed public images. My contention was, finally, that the films of this period intervene into the audience's space in a very special way. How to keep this last aspect in sight was a question that recurred again and again during the planning of the programme.

The exhilarating five days of films and lectures in September 2010 had a long prehistory. In 1989, we celebrated the tenth birthday of the Verband der Filmarbeiterinnen, the German association of women working in film, by organising short video letters. For my contribution, I sat down in front of the running camera and read from the autobiography of Alice Guy, the first woman filmmaker in movie history. For a full five minutes, I simply read out the titles of her films: LA FÉE AUX CHOUX OU LA NAISSANCE DES ENFANTS, CHARMANT FROUFROU, COUCHER D'YVETTE, MADAME A DES ENVIES, A HOUSE DIVIDED, MAKING AN AMERICAN CITIZEN, CANNED HARMONY, QUESTIONS INDIS-

---

Facing page: Cover of programme booklet designed by Maren von Stockhausen.

Lightbox with a German intertitle from Georges Méliès's À LA CONQUÊTE DU PÔLE (1912):
"The suffragettes, repudiated by the Congress, try in vain to participate in conquering the
North Pole".

CRÈTES ... . To me, the film titles pointed to an author who, between 1896 and 1920, was already telling stories from the perspective of an evidently female subjectivity. (The second wave of the women's movement, starting in the late 1960s, enthusiastically sought to 'discover', bit by bit, the lost continent of a buried and forgotten history of women auteurs; in the 1980s, that quest was replaced by debates around the feminine gaze and female authorship, and subsequently expanded into much more specific, socio-historical studies.[3] The history of the reception, identification and restoration of Alice Guy's oeuvre provides an exemplary illustration of this journey.)

In the mid-1990s, I began more detailed and systematic research on women directors from the days of silent cinema – on Lois Weber and the everyday realism of her social melodramas, Alice Guy and her insistence on a female subjectivity throughout the immense diversity of genres that she tackled, Mabel Normand and her slapstick persona at the interface between early cinema and the institution of narrative codes. While searching Henri Bousquet's *Catalogue Pathé* in the course of this research, I found many mentions of films that addressed the first-wave women's movement during its emergence at the turn of the twentieth century, often even featuring the word 'feminism' in their titles, or referring to suffragette or anti-suffragette films, to women lawyers and women doctors, to strikes by housekeepers, cooks, maids and nurses. I was struck by how extensively early film referenced the suffrage movements, and in what a wide range of different forms. Some of those allusions were implicit – such as in the many films about strikes, made around 1906, which represent the spectacle of women appearing en masse in the public space[4] both as a grotesque rabble and as a band of jaunty activists, often carrying banners in three languages.[5] Some were explicit, like the myriad films whose titles referred to the battle of the sexes, to suffragettes, feminists and women's right to vote.

These suffrage films appear in feminist film theory as early as the 1970s. In a 1972 issue of *Women and Film*,[6] Gretchen Bataille describes them as fulfilling (with very few exceptions) stereotyping functions. However, her work relies mainly on contemporary film reviews rather than analysis of the films themselves. In *Popcorn Venus* of 1973,[7] Marjorie Rosen discusses several films discrediting the movement, such as the short 1901 farce THE KANSAS CITY SALOON SMASHERS by Edwin S. Porter, in which an embittered prohibitionist and suffragette destroys a bar. Kay Sloan's 1988 study *The Loud Silents*[8] looks at the representation of political and social conflicts in early American film, and devotes a key chapter to suffragette films. Lisa Tickner's inspiring *The Spectacle of Women*, also published in 1988, addresses the suffrage movement's image production, along with propaganda, caricatures and counterpropaganda, the production of posters and the visual orchestration of demonstrations, but she makes only indirect reference to the many extant films.[9]

An initial opportunity to put my ideas into practice and expand their reach arose from my collaboration with Mariann Lewinsky on her programme *Forze irresistibili: attrici comiche e suffragettes / Irresistible Forces: Comic Actresses and Suffragettes (1910–1915)* at the 2008 Il Cinema Ritrovato festival in Bologna. I suggested adding a focus on the suffragettes to supplement the theme of comic actresses, and we were able to work through various archives together during our preparations. The suffragette films screened at that festival to some extent formed the kernel of our selection and programme design in Berlin in 2010.

The Berlin programme opened with a section entitled 'Radikale (Haus)Mädchen' (Radical Maid(en)s), the topic of which was a spectrum of different forms of radicalisation – from teenage mutiny and maidservant anarchy right up to the apparent nihilism of Robinette. The section's centrepiece was the 1913 newsreel reporting the dramatic act of radical suffragette Emily Wilding Davison, who threw herself in front of the King's horse at the Epsom Derby and was so severely injured that she died as a result. The next section, 'Militanzen' (Militancies), asked whether it was inevitable that the militancy of the British suffragette movement should have culminated in such enthusiastic nationalism when war broke out in 1914. As a *bonsoir*, we screened the anti-war film DANS LE SOUS-MARIN (1908).[10]

The next sections were 'Ein kinematographisches Studio – Inszenierung und Abbildung' (A Cinematographic Studio – Staging and Portraying), on the gendered charge of the space of mise-en-scène and its arrangements; 'Mann /

LA GRÈVE DES NOURRICES (1907).

Frau / Norm / Kino' (Man / Woman / Norm / Cinema), discussing the different manifestations of the crossdressing skirt and breeches role before and after 1910; and 'Die Frau von morgen' (The Woman of Tomorrow), named for the Russian realist melodrama of 1914, ZHENSHCHINA ZAVATRASHNEGO DNYA, which we screened after a number of short films representing women's work. For the closing section, we borrowed the title of Noël Burch's 1981 film DAS JAHR DER LEIBWACHE (*The Year of the Bodyguard*). The programme's epilogue was WORKS AND WORKERS AT DENTON HOLME, whose discontinuous, 'semi-chaotic' camera captures the cheerfulness of male and female factory workers as they look straight out at the audience.[11] And because we just couldn't stop, we added LE TORCHON BRÛLE / UNE QUERELLE DE MÉNAGE of 1911: a surreal domestic quarrel in which Rosalie and her husband argue with words and fists, can't leave each other alone and roll right down to the sewers and back in a bizarre round of parkour.

There are many facets to the theme of suffragettes when taken in such a wide-ranging sense. They include the debates around intersexuality, the photographic and cinematic representation of hysteria, the artistes and actresses of the comedy serials who initiated the 'star' concept, the incredibly large number of cinematic women who engage in physical fights, the address to a non-bourgeois cinema audience and the accomplished use of the media by the suffragette movement. Our design of the programme sections' sequences, proportions and accents was guided by a desire to reach a balance between artistic approaches to the material and approaches based on a critique of representation – we were looking for ways of calling attention to the evocative intensity of the

LA GRÈVE DES NOURRICES (1907).

films, the intelligent pleasure with which they can be consumed, their address to a heterogeneous collective of laughter, the way their physical presence spills out into the auditorium. Film-historical programmes today often neglect the materials or else fetishise them; they address highly specialised segments of the public. Yet these objects are nothing without their audience, and that audience must both be taken absolutely seriously and, indeed, also brought together in the first place. Short films tend to lead a marginal existence in cinemas. Audiences probably suspect them of being something substandard, and they still suffer from a lingering association with the primitive. Of course, badly structured programmes of short films are indescribably wearisome and demanding. Added to that, audiences nowadays often show a great resistance to tolerating the short films' considerable ambivalence, and to imagining the working-class audience of the past which they primarily address. I wanted to both highlight and combat these problems.

There is a risk that the films could be misused simply as references to a particular discourse. Avoiding this demands a light touch and skilful communication; a degree of evocative argumentation is needed to catch, for example, the roaming gaze of the recipient of art in a gallery or museum setting, someone who does not particularly like being kept sitting in a darkened room and would prefer to put together her own *petit tour*. There are, thus, stumbling blocks on all sides. With that in mind, the four films produced by the US suffragette movement itself,[12] all of them propaganda productions whose rather laboured didacticism tells us a lot about the movement's class-ridden character, interest me less than the anti-suffragette films with their startling plot constructions,[13]

PICKPOCKET (USA 1913).

and less than the photos taken secretly by the British police or the first-wave feminists' merchandising items, now being marketed on eBay in enormous quantities. I was guided by my own cinematic preferences and consideration for the audience, not by any interest in exhaustiveness, as was also indicated by the intertextual installations in the Zeughauskino foyer.[14]

There were many essential parameters for the event: generous funding by Berlin's Capital Cultural Fund, the host cinema's solidarity and commitment in giving us autonomy to draw up our programme,[15] the huge organisational effort at the venue,[16] the decision to promote the event in aesthetically divergent ways online[17] and in the programme booklet,[18] the assistance of various electronic newsletters in distributing the information.[19] By addressing and inviting not only highly specialised experts but also networks of friends and a range of young women researchers and artists, I tried to bring the project to the most diverse audience possible, as opposed to relying on the rather homogeneous world of established academia, film studies and archives.

All the programme's sections had musical accompaniment,[20] and every evening at six there were well-attended lectures on various thematic strands: on the media-savviness of the early suffragists, on the staging of hysteria in the film LA NEUROPATOLOGIA, on the use of aesthetic means to read against the grain of the hormone-research movie STEINACH-FILM, on Asta Nielsen's DIE SUF-FRAGETTE. Introducing some never-screened works made between 1900 and

'Militancies'

From 1903 on, the radical Women's Social Political Union (WSPU) fought for political rights for women in Britain under the autocratic leadership of Emmeline Pankhurst. They organised demonstrations, campaigns and countless petitions. Around 1910, the WSPU's approach took an increasingly radical turn. Their members generated publicity using militancy and violence; harsher repression ensued. Many comedies refer to the actions of the WSPU. The non-fiction films show a more orderly image, often consciously managed by the suffragettes: long marches in white garments with the insignia of Holloway Prison and well-placed placards bearing slogans like "Taxation without representation is tyranny". In LES FEMMES DÉPUTÉS (F 1912), Madame Dupont and Madame Dubois compete for election in striped ties and strict tweed suits. The film satirises the speeches, the poster fights, the electioneering among the market women and the parliamentary debates – all of which, it implies, results in babies being neglected and husbands left alone to keep house, wearing the ribbons of the Parisian wet-nurse on their top hats and meeting up with their male fellow sufferers to compare infants.

In 1918 one harassed husband still dreams of being Prime Minister and inflicting draconian punishment on suffragette activists to quash their militancy (MILLING THE MILITANTS, GB 1913), yet in fact the outbreak of the First World War saw most suffragettes rushing to serve the national cause and setting aside their demand for the right to vote. The early anti-war film DANS LE SOUS-MARIN (F 1908) ends with an allegory: the goddess of peace stands guard as all weapons are destroyed.

1905 from the Mitchell & Kenyon Collection, Vanessa Toulmin presented women's work and leisure as a poignant counterpart to the largely bourgeois suffrage movement. Mariann Lewinsky showed the work of women entertainers, the artistes and actresses; and the artist Pauline Boudry introduced her and Renate Lorenz's re-staging of Hannah Cullwick's sadomasochistic photographs.[21]

Mariann Lewinsky and I were not aiming to work through a list of every film that ever included the word "suffragette" in its title. Instead, our objective was to draw from our experiences and our shared research to create a programme that focused strongly on the representation of the subjectivities, the pugnaciousness and the artistic autonomy of women, without losing sight of the suffrage movement's class-based nature or of anti-feminist propaganda. That took knowledge, intuition, a good measure of enthusiasm and a willingness to leave some contradictions unresolved. Our shared starting point was and remains the desire to convey – and to infect others with – our enjoyment of this exuberantly experimenting cinema.

Translated from German by Kate Sturge

Notes

1. Angela McRobbie, *The Aftermath of Feminism: Gender, Culture and Social Change* (London: Sage, 2008) describes a (neo-)liberal "undoing" of feminism which takes feminism into account.

2. In its five days, the programme attracted almost 1,400 visitors from all sorts of different spheres: certainly not a single homogeneous 'scene'.

3. See, for example, Heide Schlüpmann, *The Uncanny Gaze: The Drama of Early German Cinema* (Urbana, IL: University of Illinois Press, 2010); Miriam Hansen, *Babel and Babylon: Spectatorship in American Silent Film* (Cambridge, MA: Harvard University Press, 1991); Guiliana Bruno, *Streetwalking on a Ruined Map* (Princeton, NJ: Princeton University Press, 1993); Annette Förster, *Histories of Fame and Failure. Adriënne Solser, Musidora, Nell Shipman: Women Acting and Directing in the Silent Cinema in The Netherlands, France and North America* (unpublished dissertation, University of Utrecht, 2005); Jane Gaines, "Film History and the Two Presents of Feminist Film Theory", *Cinema Journal* 44.1 (2004): 113–119.

4. In the aftermath of the 1848 revolution, political associations for "women, minors and apprentices" were banned in Prussia, for example, until 1908.

5. In French, English and occasionally also German: "Down with the Bosses", "Long Live the Strike", etc.

6. Gretchen Bataille, "Preliminary Investigations: Early Suffrage Films", *Women and Film* 1.3/4 (1974): 42–44.

7. "The pervasive male attitude toward suffrage was reflected in films." Marjorie Rosen, *Popcorn Venus: Women, Movies and the American Dream* (New York: Coward, McCann & Geoghegan, 1973), 33.

8. Kay Sloan, *The Loud Silents: The Origins of the Social Problem Film* (Urbana, IL: University of Illinois Press, 1988).

9. Lisa Tickner, *The Spectacle of Women: Imagery of the Suffrage Campaign, 1907–14* (London: Chatto & Windus, 1988).

10. See the sample from the programme booklet on the 'Militancies' section.

11. Lukas Förster, http://somedirtylaundry.blogspot.com/search?q=denton+holme (last accessed 10 May 2011).

12. VOTES FOR WOMEN (1912) with Jane Addams and Dr Anna Shaw, National American Woman

Suffrage Association (NAWSA); SUFFRAGE AND THE MAN (1912), Women's Political Union (WPU); EIGHTY MILLION WOMEN WANT – ? (1913) with Sylvia Pankhurst and Harriot Stanton Blatch (WPU); YOUR GIRL AND MINE (Selig Polyscope Company, 1914).

13. In OH! YOU SUFFRAGETTE (USA 1911), the suffragette forgets her political objectives over her fear of mice, and returns home full of remorse. In WHEN WOMEN GO ON THE WARPATH (USA 1913), the women hide their husbands' trousers to stop them going to vote. In MILLING THE MILITANTS (GB 1913), the husband – abandoned by his suffragette wife and overwhelmed by his household duties – dreams up drastic punishments reminiscent of the days of witch-hunting.

14. With the video I WOULD BE DELIGHTED TO TALK SUFFRAGE (GB 2003/2005) by Fiona Rukschcio, a panel displaying archive materials on the secret police surveillance of the suffragettes, and a lightbox containing an intertitle from Méliès's film À LA CONQUÊTE DU PÔLE (F 1912).

15. Special thanks go once again to Jörg Frieß, director of the Zeughauskino, and to Dirk Förstner, Catrin Schupke and the projectionists.

16. For our five-day programme, Dirk Förstner managed to get hold of more than eighty films from twelve European archives and distributors.

17. Website design: Claudia Heynen.

18. A 44-page booklet designed by Maren von Stockhausen.

19. For example, the notification appeared in the *KINtop* newsletter and on Luke McKernan's *Bioscope* site (see http://bioscopic.wordpress.com/2010/08/18/suffragettes-before-the-camera/; last accessed 10 May 2010), and on the lesbian sites *Konnys Lesbenseiten* and *Laura Meritt's Sexklusivitäten*.

20. Eunice Martins (piano), Stephen Horne (piano, accordion, flute) and Wieslaw Pipczynski (piano and theremin).

21. NORMAL WORK (2007), by Renate Lorenz and Pauline Boudry, performed by Werner Hirsch.

IMAGINAIRES
EN CONTEXTE (I)

DE VERBEELDING
IN CONTEXT (I)

Musée du Cinéma / Filmmuseum
Epitaaf

Eric de Kuyper

Silent Films in their First Decades – Objects for Research or for Exhibition?

for Dominique Païni

One can only agree with Michel Marie when he writes: "First of all, a film is a number in a catalogue, then a title, then an object of review in the contemporary press. After that, it becomes a film strip in an anonymous tin. *Its historical existence is limited to the discourse dedicated to it.*"[1] This "historical existence" seems to me, however, to be complete only when the film has found an audience again. Actually it exists only when it is shown before an audience on a screen; through or within a discourse, it has only a virtual existence.

★ ★ ★

I

Since the conference of the International Federation of Film Archives (FIAF) in Brighton in 1978, an entire segment of the cinema, like a lost continent, has experienced unprecedented attention and research, both intensive as well as varied. The early era, likewise the years from 1910 to 1920, which I personally call 'the second period',[2] exists thus 'in the historical sense' as and through numerous discourses. Diverse publications, magazines in many countries, festivals and retrospectives repeatedly wrest those films from oblivion. Something to rejoice about!

Nevertheless, questions still arise after a quarter century of research. I ask these questions here less as an historian[3] than as a programme planner or, as Serge Daney would have said, as *passeur*, as ferryman and smuggler. How does one bring the film into contact with an audience? How does one arrange things, so that this remarkable research accompanying the film restorations done by the cinematheques leads to a confrontation between the viewer and the films themselves, so that the films survive not only in history but also in living film culture? The results achieved in this sector are admittedly totally out of proportion to the effort involved.

Naturally, film festivals such as Le Giornate del Cinema Muto in Pordenone,

Italy, and Il Cinema Ritrovato in Bologna are duly successful. Even when the showings are widespread, with the exception of the few showings accessible to a wide audience, they reach only the small circle of specialists dedicated to 'great cinema' of the silent film era, usually the 1920s. Thus the major portion of the productions from the first decades remains an enclave reserved to historians and other specialists, where they do their careful work.

The peculiarity of the object necessarily demands that the viewers take another approach, a different attitude to cinematic theatre. Normally the films are short or of only medium length, which is why they are combined to make a 'mixed programme'. But such programmes composed of varying content contradict the expectations of the viewers, for whom an 'evening at the cinema' is synonymous with 'seeing a long film'. One is prepared to cross the line only during the course of an unusual event (for example, a festival).[4] This is not sufficient, however, as a reason for being astonished that early cinema does not succeed in taking the place it deserves among modern cineastes.

It seems important especially to show works of the 'second period' as a whole, not as fragments and selected quotations, but, of course, to perform the films on a screen as cinematic theatre. Different means have been employed to place these works in the cineaste canon, so to speak. (We could also speak of strategies, even if their use mostly happens unconsciously). One is tempted to bring this mostly little or even unknown field more in line with known fields or with those already recognised as important. For example, in 1990, the programme of the festival in Pordenone, which presented German cinema from 1910 to 1920, bore the title *Before Caligari*.[5]

Attempts to single out film makers from this era employed retrospectives and publications, the traditional method of achieving 'cinephilisation'. Yet neither Leonce Perret nor Jevgenij Bauer, neither Franz Hofer nor Alfred Machin, to name only these few, made their way into the Pantheon of the great 'auteurs'. I am not concerned whether this is absolutely necessary or only desirable; actually – and I find this fact symptomatic – those whom we consider to be the true auteurs remain basically unknown, except in specialist circles.

It seems to me that the lack of curiosity can easily be explained by the fact that the so-called cinephilia slowly but surely was based on an almost complete lack of knowledge of cinema current before the First World War. Names such as the team Louis Lumière/Georges Méliès, then D.W. Griffith in his post-Biograph phase, Louis Feuillade, Charlie Chaplin and some milestones à la CABIRIA (Giovanni Pastrone, Italy, 1914) and THE CHEAT (Cecil B. DeMille, USA, 1915) have been taken into the canon. These are examples of names and titles designated as benchmarks by the post-war generation. But at the time the cinema of the early period and the pre-war years was 'rediscovered', that is, in the last decades of the 20th century, the cineaste canon had already long since been firmly established and had been newly organized by bringing in the generation of the *politique des auteurs*, according to mechanisms which continued to function in the 'new cinephilia' as well.

The unyielding inflexibility of the cineaste precepts has led to the fact that an entire segment of cinema history has not been incorporated into the culture of film. This inflexibility has even prevented 'new auteurs' or 'new segments' from being accepted if these segments cannot be categorised using the customary orientation aids.[6] But what formed the backbone of cineaste culture in the first decades of cinema (Griffith, Lumière, Méliès and their colleagues) is much too little developed and much too inadequate to permit a system of cross references. It is easy to retrieve an Edgar G. Ulmer from oblivion by entering him into the category of *Film Noir*, to reconstruct a lineage (for example, Rainer Werner Fassbinder/Douglas Sirk/Frank Borzage) or to revive a 'sword-and-sandal' film through reference to, for example, GLADIATOR (Ridley Scott, USA, 2000). But how can Italian diva films be introduced into our film culture? Or the works of Segundo de Chomón? Or even all the anonymous, unidentified films?

★ ★ ★

In a word, we have come to a seeming dead end here. A frustrating, unnerving thought for smuggler natures such as programme planners! The thought arises from a double set of problems: On the one hand, it is fundamentally difficult to awaken cultural curiosity for a field that deserves to be rediscovered and appreciated. On the other hand, it is deeply unsatisfactory to see the classical (or new) cinephilia incapable of opening up and showing interest, which it obviously wishes to do and which it practices in its own historically limited field.

II

Therefore we in the Cinémathèque royale de Belgique (which now is called Cinematek) began to reassess the problem of the cinema in its first decades. A new evaluation seemed all the more necessary because silent films in their entire spectrum occupy an important position in the Brussels Musée du Cinéma. It had a unique showing room: a small auditorium dedicated only to silent films, where two programmes run daily (with piano accompaniment, of course).[7] We started a few studies and projects to try to give the public an innovative access to this 'unrewarding' repertory. Above all, we wanted to break the bonds of customary programming as it had been practiced in the small film room for years – even if this is an indispensible, valuable instrument for the time being. However, the viewer will too often remain the classical cineaste visitor who can disengage his or her attention from this horizon only with difficulty and turn to other works which do not correspond to the established canon or function in its context.

A first project, which we named *Imaginaires en Contexte* (Imaginations in Context), was initially thought to be an answer to the offer by the Fondation Roi Baudouin which wished to launch and support initiatives to increase the number of museum visitors. With this event series, the Cinémathèque royale de Belgique went beyond its confines and, as an extraordinary museum, offered to conduct a dialogue with the classical museums. We wanted to include barely known or totally unknown museum-like locations in Brussels into our activities and to organise showings there. We thus invited viewers/visitors to a double discovery: a forgotten museum and underestimated films.

This was by no means a new version of the rather widespread practice of showing films in unusual places, especially in touristic places, but rather a ritualistic action which naturally cares nothing about the film repertory, our chief interest. Quite the opposite, our location selection was to have a profound and characteristic connection to the programmes shown.

To make our approach better understood, I would like to describe the different events of the series in detail. The project, which took place in 1998 at the Laeken Cemetery and in the monument workshop of the Salu sculptor family, was called *La Résurrection des Images*. Along with a tour through the graves by night, the event established a link between the aesthetics of cemetery art and a film programme which followed the presentation theme or the motif of images of the saints, as is known, a frequently occurring motif in films of that era. Every tour, each about an hour long, ended directly with a film shown in the sculpture workshop of Ernest Salu and Sons. In the programme were LES DEUX PETITS JÉSUS (*The Foundling*, Georges Denola, Pathé, 1910), LE PLUS BEAU JOUR DE MA VIE (*The Most Beautiful Day of My Life*, Pathé, 1908) and ZWEIMAL GELEBT (*A Second Life*, Max Mack, Continental Kunst-Film, 1912). This 'confrontation' forced the viewer/visitor not only to consider the films within a certain context – instead of seeing them as foreign objects – but also to make this marginal art of funeral sculptures more readable and enjoyable through the projection of films which have affinities with it.

The subsequent projects dealt with other themes: AU PAYS DES TÉNÈBRES (*In the Land of Darkness*, 2000) focused on the Naturalism subject of workers and working conditions with AU PAYS NOIR (*Tragedy in a Coal Mine*, Ferdinand Zecca, Pathé, 1905), LA GRÈVE (*Strike*, Ferdinand Zecca, Pathé, 1904), LA VEUVE DU MARIN (*The Sailor's Widow*, Pathé, 1907) and HET GEHEIM VAN HET STAAL (*The Secret of Steel*, Alfred Machin, Hollandsche, 1912). The performance occurred in the studio of the painter and sculptor Constantin Meunier (1831–1905). The subject of working conditions, widespread in early cinema, is here reflected in the works of a contemporary artist who dedicated his entire output to this subject.

A third project, *Les Ailes du temps* (The Wings of Time, 2002), concerned a further motif which the *Belle Époque* was obsessed with: flying. There could not have been a better place for the showings than the grand hall of the Brussels Cinquantenaire Park, namely, the hall of the Musée de l'Armée, devoted to the history of aeronautics. Together with MAUDITE SOIT LA GUERRE (*War Be Damned*, Alfred Machin, Belge-Cinéma-Film 1913), topicals of the Gaumont Company were shown.

Following the revival of *La Résurrection des Images* at the Campo Santo Cemetery in Ghent, the last project *Phantasmes* (Illusions, 2004)) was organised within the walls of the Musée Guislain. It was dedicated to the history of 'madness'. The films UN RAGNO NEL CERVELLO (*Spider on the Brain*, Emilio Vardannes, Itala Film, 1912) and LE RETAPEUR DE CERVELLES (*Brains Repaired*, Emile Cohl, Pathé, 1911) were followed by LE MYSTÈRE DES ROCHES DE KADOR (*The Mystery of the Rocks of Kador*, Léonce Perret, Gaumont 1912).[8]

Additional projects in Brussels are scheduled with a programme of *Chinoiserie and Japanaiserie* (in the Japanese Tower of the Chinese Pavillion), the neo-rococo (in the Vauxhall of the Parc de Bruxelles) and *Artist Life* (in the Mommen art workshop and in the Musée Charlier). As can be seen, there is no lack of ideas. But the costs are a heavy burden on the museums. Additionally, unusual efforts have been demanded of the project partners (opening their houses at uncustomary hours, cinema in small rooms or ill-suited locations for the projection etc.), all of which was, however, rewarded by the enthusiasm and the reactions of the audience.[9]

To facilitate a direct confrontation between place and film showing, the films ran without any introduction. However, all of the projects provided an accompanying brochure in which specialists, conservators from the participating museums and film historians offered advisory services. To name only the film historians: Mariann Lewinsky, Heide Schlüpmann, Edwin Carels, Marc Holthof, Marc-Emmanuel Melon and Dirk Lauwaert wrote articles for the publications.[10]

As can be seen, the selected locations are striking and significant examples of the culture of the 19th century. My proposition is, namely, that early cinema is deeply rooted in the culture of that century, and that is why it is there that we must look for the key to understanding these films and for the key to the possibilities of making it accessible to an audience. The English historian Eric J. Hobsbawm formulated for general history that the 19th century lasted beyond the First World War.[11] This idea applies to cinema as well, which, as already mentioned, emerged in the 20th century, yet reflected very little of that century.

This assessment explains, on the other hand, the difficulty which the cineaste audience can have with these films. They evidently speak a different 'language' from that of the cinema that the audience knows and loves, films which, moreover, treat 'out-dated' topics in a naïve manner... Doubtless the distinctly sentimental character, the Manichaeism in the behaviour of the personae, the pronounced theatricality lie far beyond our aesthetic criteria. In a word, this cinema has not arrived into the modern era.[12] In the 1920s, the first cineastes also shared this opinion and could not appreciate pre-war cinema as cinema of another century, except for the above-mentioned few films. Even if this can be explained and understood in the post-war context, this lack of respect had grave consequences for the development of the cineaste canon and the culture of film.

Imaginaires en Contexte runs totally in a different direction: it emphasises, namely, the aesthetic context and the mentality of the 19th century, one which was characterised by aesthetics different from those of the post-war period. Instead of adapting the cinema to the 20th century and a cinephilia which is not capable of an adoption, we put it into the ambience where it fits. We linked it to the circumstances of the 19th century, which we carefully selected to stimulate a dialogue between cinema and art (or culture), so to speak.

In all modesty, we suggest a different viewpoint, a modified history of film! As the context of the 20th century does not fit these works, we are giving them another, one better suited to them, a context from the 19th century. As a museum object, the body of the film can again function. As we will see, *Imaginaires en Contexte* with its new way of presentation will additionally fulfil another modern need.

III

It was truly remarkable to see how a wide audience flocked to the *Imaginaires en Contexte* showings and were enthusiastic about films which they would not have gone to see in the cinema (for example, to the cinema in the Brussels Musée du Cinéma). Had they seen the films in the cinema, the audience would not have appreciated the films in the same way as happened in our perform-ances. In the cinema of the Musée du Cinéma, these films exist more or less as (cinematographic) objects of research; with *Imaginaires en Contexte*, which offers the idea of an event, the films once again become (cinematographic) performances. The films became that literally, for the works never had this status for the viewers, not even virtually through cinephilia.

At this point, we should consider the culture of cinema within the broader framework in which it inevitably belongs. For example, a continuing, even radical, reversal in the direction of a different kind of 'cultural consumption' can be observed (the word 'consumption' has not been used incidentally!). If the classical or contemporary cinephilia moves mainly in an ambience of 'historical knowledge', then the various methods of acquisition of culture are characterised and delineated rather in terms and categories of '(cultural or viewer) experience'. The acquisition or simply the cultural practice is deter-mined by the intensity of what those concerned experienced and the *event* aspect of culture. For example, the sociologist Gerhard Schulze suggests we no longer call our societal type "société du spectacle" (society of the spectacle, Guy Debord); he expands the perspective by renaming it and analyses it as the "event culture".[13]

It is as if cultural events which earlier took place in a more or less solid framework of continuity and transformation and thus functioned in institu-tional spaces were now taking on a distinct feature marking them as events, even when they retained their characteristics for the most part. An event is, so to speak, fundamentally anti-institutional; an institution in its basic sense is counter to the idea of event. However, to survive, the institutions must follow present-day taste and embrace events.

For example, art museums are focusing on large retrospectives and special exhibitions rather than on their own collections – unless the museum structure itself is considered an event, as do the Guggenheim in Bilbao or the Centre Georges Pompidou in Paris and the classical tourist centres, the Louvre in Paris and the Prado in Madrid. That also explains the increase in festivals of all kinds, a major component of the tourist industry. Festivals, of their very nature, are beyond the customary and the everyday and therefore are already endowed with 'event character'.

That is, we seem to perceive culture only through the event scrim; this applies to cinema culture as well. The other aspect of the phenomenon is equally important: the role of the media in the functioning of the arts. For only through events can media interest be secured, and the media are also dependent on cultural life.

The information media do not report the activities of institutions but hunger after the dramatic attraction emanating from these institutions. The (cultural) event feeds the media and conversely. Only the sensational winds up in the media. They are not interested in institutional culture unless it has reached the level of event, which is what all cultural establishments aspire to. That seems to them the best survival strategy, which is why the decline of the institutions is linked to the emergence of the event culture. Even such a traditional institution as a university feels itself forced to follow the rules of the market and to represent the acquisition of knowledge as a transaction between producer and consumer. Market ideology has ploughed the field of culture, namely into the direction of the 'eventful'.

Incidentally, traditional cinephilia as well is locked in a crisis, as it focuses too much on historical knowledge, whereas the so-called new cinephilia adds an essential dimension, a practice linked to the intensive use of the new media. Going to the cinematheque or to the repertory cinema (with all the attendant and resulting conventions) is something different from collecting, exchanging, searching for and watching DVDs! There, the manipulation/consumption by means of the media is an integral element of the activities; they are part of the passion itself.[14]

Here is the hope of better understanding why early silent films are not accepted by cineastes or film culture, but they are indeed qualified to function in our event culture – if they are adequately presented as event. Such a situation may be regrettable, but there is no getting past this recognition. And an important element is added: the opportunity of lending this cinema a 'spectacular' framework because circulation via the new media (which the new cinephilia espouses) permits only scholarly approach. Naturally, this opportunity demands of the programme planners and the 'smugglers' a method not oriented toward continuity (the institution: the cinema hall with its daily screenings) but toward a use with ever new demands based on discontinuity (the event cannot be the everyday).

The event-oriented not only does not exclude increased attention but, on the contrary, demands research work into the historical and the aesthetic, a genuine affinity with the idea of 'spectacle' . . . and, above all, an adequate budget. Here it can be seen that at least the search for the attractive form in this field coincides with a serious concern for the contents.

IV

The musical accompaniment represents a significant element in silent films. The almost monthly telecasts of silent films on the German-French TV station ARTE would not be possible without the addition of a musical backdrop. It was also found for screenings in a cinema that the presence of at least a pianist was absolutely necessary for every silent film performance.

Indeed, the musical accompaniment for the films is imperative but extraordinarily precarious at the same time. A successful musical backdrop not only supports and comments on the film but enriches and fleshes it out, all the while remaining in the shadows. The 'music' (and the musician/s) leads the viewers not only through the projected film – the music understands, experiences and translates it; it also gives support. If, however, the accompaniment does not play its role as mediator, it falsifies the film, makes it difficult to understand, boring etc. Instead of giving support, the music clouds the viewer's attention. This is not only a matter of discretion, for this can end in monotone neutrality. On the other hand, too much expressivity harbours the risk of being intrusive and irritating for appreciating the film. The right measure must be found – with improvisation, that depends for the most part on the musicians' emotional relationship to the film and on their mood on that particular evening. It is this very risk that makes the silent film accompanied by *live* music an experience and enables this kind of cinema to become (again) a genuine, vivid spectacle. It is all the more peculiar that in-depth considerations on the role and function of music in silent films or on its aesthetics do not exist as far as I know.[15]

★ ★ ★

And, in fact, *live* silent film performances have become numerous. We should not underestimate the work that David Gill, Kevin Brownlow and Carl Davis contributed in the 1980s for the presentation of longer silent films with orchestral accompaniment. Since that time, the operating experience with reconstructed original scores has greatly increased, including commissioned works by composers today and, unfortunately as well, with an endless number of musicians who, under the pretext of accompanying the film, overindulge in the pleasures of 'making their own music'. Not only does the quality of these endeavours often suffer, but we also see unimaginative film selection. The avant-garde of the 1920s, Sergei Eisenstein and a few films by Friedrich Wilhelm Murnau, seem to be consistent with the limited inspiration of the musicians.

However, it must be admitted that this meagre offering has brought a wider audience to these works and that these activities fit perfectly with the above-mentioned demand for event culture. The organisers of traditional concerts also sense the need to make their programmes more attractive by adding a visual

Das Stahlwerk der Poldihütte (Sascha, 1916).

element. For example, arbitrary experiments have occurred such as a *concert performance* of Sergei Prokofiev's score to Aleksandr Nevskij performed with a *silent* showing of this sound film (Sergej Eisenstein, Soviet Union, 1938)! And that is not nearly the extent of such regrettable attempts to combine film and music, totally without a sense of their special interaction which makes up the heart and soul of this silent art ... .

The Cinémathèque royale de Belgique is cooperating on a project with the Orchestre National de Belgique and the Palais des Beaux-Arts to satisfy the genuine need for a renewal of the concert ritual but also to take the opportunity of intensifying and enriching showings of silent films which do not belong to the repertory. Important is the aspect of creation, not illustration: we offer an audience the unexpected encounter of music and film and, at the same time, offer them the opportunity, parallel to discovering surprising dimensions of a piece of music, of becoming acquainted with an unknown silent film and thus altering concert art a bit as well. This gamble is all the riskier but also the more exciting because the project's film is unknown to the audience; moreover, it is a documentary whose origins are still unclear and which thus far only a small group of specialists has seen. This documentary from 1916 is called Das Stahlwerk der Poldihütte während des Weltkriegs (*The Poldihütte Steelworks during the World War*), produced by Sascha-Film (Vienna).[16] This almost 50-minute documentary 'describes' a steel mill and weapons factory with images of such impact and severity that they are in hard contrast to historical reality. They stem from the First World War. Observed from an objective distance as with the eyes of an entomologist, this place is shown producing the bombs for the massive annihilation taking place on the front at the same time.

DAS STAHLWERK DER POLDIHUETTE (Sascha, 1916).

Without doubt, DAS STAHLWERK DER POLDIHÜTTE can be classified as a propaganda film,[17] but it confuses and surprises through its distanced approach, avoiding any grandiloquent affectation.

The beauty of the images of architecture and industrial landscape,[18] the unhurried rhythm of the sequences, the somnambulatory interaction between the workers and their surroundings, all this is presented as a hermetically closed universe. All these qualities make of this document a grandiose moment of non-fictional cinema. In light of our historical knowledge and awareness of the fact that this lustrous world is the reverse of the bloody massacre playing out only a few hundred miles away, the film is all the more harsh and 'unbearable' to the eyes of today's viewer.

But who are these viewers? They are hard to find, except for constantly the same specialists like us! The potential audience remains unreachable. It cannot be expected that an unexciting programme with an unknown film from 1916, and a non-fictional one at that, is going to attract many viewers. And, yet, this film merits a large audience, says the smuggler! With a showing on the large screen which would bring out the cinematic qualities in a large screening room. Hence it requires a strong argument to carry this out.

A musical composition is indispensible as a response to the effort made for a cinema screening. It is not an illustration: the unbearable character – the unsaid in DAS STAHLWERK DER POLDIHÜTTE – is to be made apparent by means of the musical discourse. As the war is the core of the unsaid, it seemed appropriate to select from one of the violence-imbued works. Thus Dmitri Shostakovich

DAS STAHLWERK DER POLDIHÜTTE (Sascha, 1916).

sprang immediately to mind as the composer. His *Symphony No. 8* (in C minor, opus 65), composed in 1943 while the Battle of Stalingrad raged (the work is at times accorded this title), contrasts completely with DAS STAHLWERK DER POLDIHÜTTE. This "immense oratory without words about terror and death", as one critic wrote, visualizes what the images hide or simply presuppose: the violence, the desperation in the face of the massacre among Men. Through the suggestive power of the music, each grenade is transformed into a coffin! Admittedly, the film is about a different war – a film about the First World War with music about the Second World War. Yet, as a cynic might say, the ability to destroy and to cause suffering has hardly changed. Shostakovich's work was also selected to permit a non-narrative, contrasting discourse which would unmask the cheerful images and to place them – concretely, physically, almost into the raw viscera – in a context the viewer could grasp, without the music, only in an intellectual and abstract way.

The idea of a concert that becomes a spectacle is important to us. Thanks to its length, the symphony can already be heard before the showing begins, as an overture or prologue. After about twenty minutes, the images appear, as has been said, images of an innocent purity whose horror we can grasp only later. But thanks to the music, this recognition does not occur in retrospect but simultaneously owing to the constant tension between the frantic intensity of the music and the beauty of the images.

This film represents more than a film accompanied by music. It is an independent creation employing works from two different areas permitting a new discourse to arise from their confrontation. The premiere took place in the

Henri Lebœuf concert-hall of the Palais des Beaux-Arts in Brussels in the spring of 2006, with the Orchestre National de Belgique conducted by Hartmut Haentchen.

It is certainly no coincidence that it is productions of the forgotten years and not those of the great period of silent film in the 1920s which force us to find new ways to reach an audience by means of a different perspective closer to the expectations of our own time. This repertory can find a second life by being shown in a rather 'spectacular' framework and not simply in a cinema, by furnishing it with the attraction of being an event.

Translated from German, based on the original French text, by Frankie Kann

Notes

Eric de Kuyper's contribution was first published in German: "Der Stummfilm der ersten Jahrzehnte – Studiengegenstand oder Schauobjekt?", *KINtop* 14/15 (2006): 137-150.

1. Italics in French text. Michel Marie, "Introduction" in André Gaudreault (ed.), *Pathé 1900. Fragments d'une filmographie analytique du cinema des premiers temps* (Sainte Foy/Paris: Presses de l'Université de Laval/Presses de la Sorbonne Nouvelle, 1993), 6.

2. Eric de Kuyper. "Le cinema de la seconde époque: le muet des années dix", *Cinématheque* 1 and 2 (1992): 28–36 and 58–68.

3. Historiography is not my occupation, but, through my work for the Nederlands Filmmuseum and through my connections with the Cinémathèque royale de Belgique, I am more or less forced to take the historical standpoint.

4. The pattern of viewing long feature films has been altered by television, where fragmentation and seriality are accepted. This is why films from this era suit to compilation works or programme montages. The examples in this field are numerous, and most of the films are of high quality. To name only a few: UN MONDE AGITÉ (Alain Fleischer, France, 2000), LYRISCH NITRAAT (Peter Delpeut, Netherlands, 1991), DIVA DOLOROSA (Peter Delpeut, Netherlands, 1999).

5. I had a bit of fun with this in my article "La griffe des auteurs", *Art Press*, Special No. 14 (1993): 58–64). See also my text on the good and bad use of the idea of influence: "Du bon et du mauvais usage de la notion d'influence", *Cinémathèque* 4 (1993): 15–21.

6. A rule in Information Theory demands that every message with new content must be linked to a strong message and must be recognised in public opinion or by the recipient.

7. After the reconstruction of the Musée du Cinéma, there are still two theatres, but none is exclusively devoted to silent film screenings which take place in the big auditorium as well as in the small theatre.

8. This programme was also shown in the Narrenturm in Vienna on the occasion of the international conference Film Geschichte Schreiben (Writing the history of film) from 1–4 April 2004. It should be noted that it was possible to introduce non-Western film cultures into the canon and into present-day cinema. However, other criteria and other cultures – extra-cinematographic – reference points were present or were at least accessible. The only starting point in respect to films before the First World War, it seems to me, is their link to the culture and aesthetics of the previous century, as a growing interest for this period might be expected.

9. Only 35-mm prints were shown, accompanied by piano, with the exception of the programmes lent to Ghent, where, due to costs, the films were shown using DVDs. The experience gained there was not conclusive, however. The offer normally encompassed six showings, with two showings each per evening at long weekends which ran 60 minutes and were combined with a visit of the location.

10. The editors organised a day of study each with invitations for the collaborators who were to compose the articles. They were to view a film programme in the Brussels Cinémathèque containing more titles than those to be shown in the later event. They were also able to visit the location of the showing. In this way, we hope to bring the specialists from the diverse fields to a

first exchange, one occurring much too seldom among the various disciplines. For both parties, the film specialists as well as the specialists of the museums, this encounter proved to be very valuable, as for example some film material could be identified or museum specialists discovered unknown footage from their collections.

11. Eric J. Hobsbawm speaks of the "long 19th century" in his *The Age of Empire* (London: Weidenfeld and Nicolson, 1987), 6. His book *The Age of Extremes* (London: Michael Joseph, 1994) which he devoted to the 20th century is subtitled "The Short 20th Century".

12. I have emphasised this repeatedly, for example, the curious lack of art nouveau in the films produced at the time of this aesthetic movement: Eric de Kuyper. "Alla ricerca delle trace dell'Art Nouveau e del Simbolismo nel cinema dei primi decenni" in Gianpiero Brunetta (ed.), *Storia del cinema mondiale*, Vol. 1 (Turin: Einaudi, 1999), 176–197.

13. Gerhard Schulze, *Die Erlebnisgesellschaft. Kultursoziologie der Gegenwart* (Frankfurt am Main: Carl Hanser, 1992).

14. On the significance of the tactile dimension of this practice cf. Emile Poppe, "Vers une digitalisation du visual?" in Alice Autelitano, Veronica Innocenti and Valentina Re (eds), *I cinque sensi del cinema* (Udine: Forum, 2005), 49–52.

15. Whereas many books exist about music in sound films, the offer concerning the aesthetics of music for silent films is all the more meagre, apart from studies dedicated solely to techniques and history. One exception, however, can be named here: Emilio Sala, *L'opera senza canto. Il mélo romantico e l'invenzione della Colonna Sonora* (Venice: Marsilio), 1995.

16. Elisabeth Büttner, Christian Dewald, *Das tägliche Brennen. Eine Geschichte des österreichischen Films von den Anfängen bis 1945* (Salzburg/Vienna: Residenz Verlag, 2002), 140–145.

17. Is it a propaganda film? A justifiable question. According to Tom Gunning, the non-fictional film altered its character during the First World War; the documentary arose from the 'view' aesthetic. DAS STAHLWERK DER POLDIHÜTTE fits wonderfully into the 'view' aesthetic, not, however, into that of the documentary film. See Tom Gunning, "Vor dem Dokumentarfilm. Frühe *non-fiction Filme* und die Ästhetik der 'Ansicht'", *KINtop* 4 (1995): 111–121. On the unclear status of German propaganda film, cf. Oskar Messter, "Der Film als politisches Werbemittel", printed in *KINtop* 3 (1993): 93–103.

18. Prepared for possible self-criticism (see note 5), I would compare DAS STAHLWERK DER POLDI-HÜTTE with the industrial architecture photos by Bernd and Hilla Becher.

MITCHELL & KENYON
ELECTRIC EDWARDIANS
EAST LANCASHIRE ON FILM

Rare archive film of Blackburn, Darwen, Accrington, Burnley and beyond
Footage by pioneering Blackburn film-makers presented by Dr Vanessa Toulmin
of the University of Sheffield, with live piano accompaniment by Stephen Horne
Supported by the Heritage Lottery Fund in aid of the "Empire100 Raise the Roof Appeal"

EMPIRE
ESTD THEATRE 1910

WEDNESDAY
17th MARCH

10am & 2pm Free Schools Performance - Please Book In Advance
2pm: Monday Club Members £2.50 | 7:30pm: Public Showing - £7 (£6 Balcony)
BOX OFFICE 01254 685500
www.thwaitesempiretheatre.co.uk

Vanessa Toulmin

Programming the Local:
Mitchell & Kenyon and the Local Film Show

Introduction

The Mitchell & Kenyon Collection is now the third largest film collection in the world relating to the output of a single company from the early 1900s. The Collection was donated to the British Film Institute in 2000 by Peter Worden a local businessman in Blackburn who rescued the films, and was researched by the University of Sheffield. Books, articles and DVDs have been produced on the Collection, and thousands of copies of the DVDs have been sold.[1] The films have been shown at international film festivals, resulted in international media coverage and produced numerous articles. Shortly after its discovery and subsequent restoration by the BFI, Mitchell & Kenyon became nationally and internationally renowned and soon became the most important early film material in the national collection of BFI National Archives. Millions of people have seen the films on television and in venues from Pordenone to San Francisco, Leeds to Luxembourg and Blackburn to Boston, over half a million cinema-goers have watched the films. The films have moved from the film festival and the archival presentation format to becoming part of Youtube on the BFI's own channel, music festivals with bands such as Lemon Jelly and *In The Nursery* combining modern music to the films and part of contemporary art installations.[2]

On a historical level the collection is now a treasure trove of international importance that reveals snapshots of the working class at work and play, watching football (both association and rugby), participating in civic and religious events; and enjoying a range of other leisure activities. Individually these lost and forgotten films can be described as tiny vignettes capturing fragments of larger more complex events, the archaeology of early film technique now available for us to study. However, Mitchell & Kenyon the collection does not necessarily tell the whole story of the material that is found within. In reality, the collection is actually a mishmash of surviving material taken from hundreds of different early film programmes commissioned or programmed in the early 1900s for local audiences by different showmen working for or in association with the company. The images that now gaze out

---

Facing page: Flyer for *East Lancashire on Film*, Thwaites Theatre, Wednesday 17 March 2010.

to us a century later have become many things but at their heart they are essentially local records unique to the town or city in which they were captured. This article tells the story of how the films were re-animated and programmed for a modern audience outside the film festivals and academic conferences but taken back to the places they originally captured on film a century ago. From 2005 onwards an estimated 20,000 people have seen the films in their home town. Over 130 local shows have been presented with often repeat viewings with Sheffield for example booking the show at least five times.

Local films

Local films are not unique to the Mitchell & Kenyon Collection, in fact you could say that the only unique aspect about the Collection initially was the sheer quantity of local films discovered, (some 838 reels) and the astonishing visual quality of the material taken from original nitrate negatives. Local films abound in archives throughout the world both locally, regionally and nationally. In the United Kingdom the local films is at the heart of the regional film archiving collection policies and in the United States, the local film has become an important part of the AMIA community both in terms of research, exhibition and collections.[3] In the early period, the local film was something that early cinema historians had always known about and although it has aroused very important recent academic scrutiny, on the whole this type of material was seen as merely a footnote in the canon of film scholarship.[4]

However, to the regional film archives in the United Kingdom, the local has always been more than just a stepping stone, it is often the means by which an archive could engage with its public, as people became increasingly occupied with and obsessed by the history of their families, their houses and their towns. The emotional impact aroused by these types of films was always the cry of recognition from the audience when familiar images of their town or city or village were screened. Therefore, the issue of how to programme some 28 hours of non fiction footage that was itself remnants of incomplete programmes was found within current regional archival practice and also within Mitchell & Kenyon's original marketing practice of 'Local Films For Local People'.

'Local films for Local People' was the key advertising phrase that both the film company and the exhibitors used in marketing their shows. The popularity of the local in the early 1900s was also prevalent in the written record with the reporter for the *Showman* newspaper commenting in 1902 that 'the public taste for animated pictures is as strong as ever, but it is the skilful treatment of local event that does much towards filling the building every night'.[5] Local newspapers from the 1900s also abound with descriptions of the film shows as being 'greatly attractive', 'a good drawer', and 'nothing is as good as a local film to attract the public'.[6] A hundred years on, this phrase provided the key to how the material could once again be revealed to what was and still is the core audience for the collection – local people. It was decided that if it worked so

Professor Vanessa Toulmin presents *Central Lancashire on Film*, Grand Theatre Blackpool, 13 January 2008

effectively for the showmen perhaps it would work as well if not better a century later.

From 2005 onwards the National Fairground Archive in association with the British Film Institute instigated a series of film programmes relating to highlighting the local films in the Mitchell & Kenyon Collection. The first twelve shows were often taken from the core programme which became the DVD release with one or two additional local titles, but as demand increased from 2005 onwards, the touring collection criss-crossed the country.[7] Weekly films in a variety of locations were presented, in the style of an Edwardian exhibition, with musical accompaniment and a lecturer to explain the films. These shows often opened in the same venues and were often the same titles that would have been exhibited a century before.

These exhibitions rapidly became a process of exchange and communication as the local people provided intimate knowledge of the area and its stories that brought the material to life and also became involved in where and how the films were shown in their locality. These programmes became more adventurous and became specifically programmed shows tailored to the local needs and commissioned by curators, programmers, local film societies and local authorities who saw in this material a means by which civic pride could be celebrated or commemorated. The local shows became the highlight of the Mitchell & Kenyon project and it became apparent that the audience needed to feel part of the performance.

Programming the local

The original *Electric Edwardians* show reel complete with live commentary, took place in Leeds, Cork, Sheffield, Derby, Edinburgh, Bristol, Glasgow, Belfast, Dublin, Manchester, Preston, Leicester, Stoke, Lancaster, Carlisle, Birmingham, Hull and other towns and cities, with audience participation being a memorable feature of each show. Following on from the practice of the original showmen in the 1900s this core programme also featured four or five titles unique to each town the films were presented. The local films became the main feature of the presentation as the audience waited in anticipation for their locality to be shown on screen. Faces, places and lost buildings were brought to life not only by the images on screen but also throughout each screening through the local response and knowledge. These sessions were good opportunities to acquire additional information about the films. Locations were always familiar to the local audience, churches were named, streets and roads identified and the trajectory of the journey or angle filmed by Mitchell & Kenyon was as marvellous to the modern viewer as it would have been to the Edwardian audience.

The original *Electric Edwardians* tour had marketed aspects of the local films within the core programme but it was not until 2006 that it was decided to programme whole shows whenever possible relating to the entirely of local material relevant to a town or a region. Regional programmes were initially put together including East Lancashire on Film, Central Lancashire on Film, North Lancashire on Film, South Yorkshire on film. Towns and cities that had enough material to bring together a seventy minute film programme were then given their own specialist show and these included Manchester and Liverpool on Film.

Wherever possible for this specialist local shows attempts were made to present the films in the original location and the shows became a partnership with the local film societies or the local history groups that wanted to see all of the material that related to their town. One of the highlights of the touring shows took place in Chorley in 2006. The Chorley Electric Palace built in 1911 was the original venue where the films were once presented as part of the Coronation celebrations and 400 people packed into two sell out shows to see views of local mills, church exits and the 1911 Coronation celebrations.

Sheffield was once again seen in its pre-war splendour before the 1960s development changed the city and reactions ranged from amazement at the splendour of the Edwardian cities to shock at seeing thousands of mill girls with their heads covered in East Lancashire. A rendition of the old football chant 'who ate all the pies' rang out from the audience in Sheffield as their former goalkeeper William 'Fatty' Foulkes once again patrolled the nets at Bramall Lane. Sometimes the films appeared particularly topical with the footage of the women factory workers covering their head and faces with large shawls striking a cord with the audience with parallels drawn on the issue of British Asian girls and the hijab. The North Lancashire show saw half the audience identify a previously unknown factory exit as Vickers and Maxims of Barrow-in-Furness, with the railway bridge in Doncaster recognised as being the exit from the Great Northern Railway works.

This is a local show

After two years of touring the collection a significant change became apparent in the audience reception and the manner in which the material was being programmed by the venues. The films were suddenly being used for a variety of reasons ranging from local anniversaries, civic occasions and a means of involving the community in matters of local importance. Greater audience involvement became a feature of these very localised shows and this became instigated by the audience and the bookers in each individual locality. My role changed to that of impresario and producer as I was called on to programme the films for a variety of rationales. Rotherham Labour Party sponsored a screening with local MP Dennis McShane co-presenting and publicised the show as a fundraiser for the forthcoming elections in the area. The Manchester screenings were different again, when students from the Northern College of Music worked with the Cornerhouse Cinema to produce a day of material relating purely to Manchester. Three hours of material relating to Manchester survived in the Collection and a series of workshop screenings were held where the students choose the films they wished to perform to and then my role was to programme this material into a narrative form. The programme was divided into four sections comprising 'Workers', 'High Days and Holidays', 'Civic Occasions and Sport' with musical accompaniment ranging from a twenty piece orchestra to a quartet for each group section. Over 50 students took part in the show held on the 4 March 2007 and 800 people attended the screenings.[8]

Civic pride soon became the rationale for the longer more locally programmed material and certain highlights stand out from the shows presented. Blackpool Council in 2007 launched its heritage and culture strategy to demonstrate that Blackpool's visual and entertainment history was worthy in international inclusion in the World Heritage registrar. They commissioned the University of Sheffield to curate a programme that would highlight their Victorian heritage and a specially invited audience of 800 people watched the films presented at the 1894 Frank Matcham designed Victorian variety theatre. Popular demand resulted in an additional weekend of local films held in conjunction with the North West Film Archive and the BFI and the story of Blackpool on Film was narrated over a weekend in January 2008 and attended by over 1200 people.[9]

Local rivalries and knowledge became an essential part of the narrative written for each regional show. The audience expected the narrator to know the essential parts of their history and street names, important historical and architectural landmarks had to be noticed and explained but with enough left out to allow the audience to be part of the proceedings. For example, the Blackpool show contained an eight minute tram ride from Blackpool to

Lytham from 1903 on the newly opened tram line which is still used today. The audience were invited to shout out and name the landmarks shown on screen and it was decided to only correct the audience if they were wrong.

The importance of knowing when to incorporate local knowledge became as important as the films that were selected as it was imperative to keep something back in order to allow for the audience to feel that they were contributing to the films but not to interrupt the flow of the programme. Perhaps the most difficult show took place in my home towns of Morecambe and Lancaster in 2006 and 2007 where I was expected to know every single detail of the material presented with my extended family in the audience. Morecambe Winter Gardens was both the setting and the original venue for the showing of the Morecambe material and it was poignant that the films were used as a fundraiser to enable them to save the Victorian variety theatre from destruction. The forty minute programme was repeated on the hour four times in a semi derelict building site with a sheet for a screen, a local DVD projector donated by a charity shop and an amateur pianist enthusiastically accompanying the films and often drowning out my narration. The film programme was then exhibited in the nearby city of Lancaster a year later and of all the shows curated this was perhaps the most problematic as local rivalries became an issue on the evening. One individual in the audience became increasingly disruptive as I presented the films and it soon became a two way conversation between myself and the amateur historian in the audience who interrupted the narrative on various occasions. After the fifth of such interventions my mother turned round to the individual and told them to shut up and informed the individual that my father's family were Lancastrians of a thousand years standing and as his daughter I was more than qualified to narrate the town's history. This view was endorsed by ringing applause from the auditorium, but it highlighted the issues one had to face when presenting such locally specific material. After this experience I took to including a preface to the show by inviting individuals to discuss any issues after the show and not to interrupt the performance.

Liverpool on film

Civic pride was again the rationale behind the largest show held since the launch in January 2005 in Blackburn when over 1000 people came to the St George's Hall as part of Liverpool Capital of Culture in May 2008. The two Liverpool shows provide an interesting lesson to the film programmer and demonstrated the importance of bringing the local people on board in the organisation and marketing of the programme. The original *Electric Edwardians* tour featuring one or two titles was programmed in May 2005 by the local independent cinema and resulted in the smallest audience for the shows as the programmer had made little or no attempt to involve the local audience and expected the power of the recent television series to arouse interest. This was a major mistake and lessons were learnt from this experience. All future local shows, from then on, relied on on local history societies, media outlets and radio stations in highlighting to the audience the local nature of the material on offer. In 2008, the lessons learnt from three years of touring shows came together in a specially commissioned *Liverpool on Film* event organised by the City of Culture Company with the University of Liverpool. Organised in partnership with Dr Julia Hallam from the School of Architecture, the show was advertised as presenting the Edwardian splendour of the city, capturing its heyday as the port of the Empire.[10] In addition the magnificent Grade 1 listed St George's Hall was used for the show as it was the original venue where the material had been seen in 1901. The material was selected to bring maximum emotional intensity to the evening and instead of showing the films chronologically, the two hours of surviving material was programmed into a narrative which told the story of the city in the early part of the 1900s. Starting with "Life in the City", followed by "Processions and Pageantry" the programme progressed to "Sport and Leisure" and ended with shots of the Liverpool skyline as the Cunard ocean liners left the dock. With piano and flute accompaniment by Stephen Horne, the music was a mixture of contemporary material and songs relevant to the people of Liverpool. For example with the football films it was decided to use the Liverpool anthem 'You'll Never Walk Alone' from the Roger and Hammerstein's musical *Carousel* instead of a contemporary song. This song has become indentified with the Kop from the 1960s and is sung at every match played by Liverpool. As the football films on the whole feature large panning shots of the crowd, a song associated primarily with the fans was more in keeping it was felt than contemporary music or modern improvisation. The final five minute sequence was presented with no accompanying narrative but solely by Stephen Horne playing the Edwardian folk song 'The Leaving of Liverpool' firstly on piano and then fading out to a flute solo as the song was repeated. Over 1000 people attended the screening which was prolifically advertised in the city in the weeks leading up to the event with selected highlights shown on large screens in the city centre. After the show, Stephen told me that we would never have been allowed to use those songs or programme format at the National Film Theatre as we had split up titles, played anachronistic music, and curated the show as a modern performance piece rather than a historical recreation. I responded by explaining that this was a local show for local people and as such required a particular style of programming that was relevant to the knowledge and experience of the audience. Descriptions of film edits, panning shots and observations relating to technique were not part of the script but facts and figures relating to the city of Liverpool, its local economy and background to the events on screen were more what the audience wished to hear.

Local show for local children in Blackburn

Perhaps the most astonishing level of local participation occurred in March 2010 when three specially programmed events were held to celebrate the 100 anniversary of the local theatre in Blackburn. Three special screenings including two for local primary schools were held from 10am onwards and the theatre worked with the local schools to make this an extraordinary event. As the doors

Local Blackburn school children wave to the camera in the manner of the Mitchell & Kenyon films, 17 March 2010.

opened, a crocodile line of children dressed in Edwardian costumes paraded into the theatre and over 400 children between the ages of six years old to eight sat patiently in the theatre. Thwaites theatre working in conjunction with the local schools had arranged for the children to be involved in the screening by encouraging them to dress up in the clothes from the time and a competition was held to see who was the most authentic. In addition the children also re-enacted some of the films on screen and had made their own movie echoing the films of St Barnabas School parading through the streets of Blackburn in 1905. The final part of the project was to watch the films at the theatre and then to complete their movie by promenading from the theatre back to their local school, all of which was to be captured on film. The local film has returned a hundred years on since they were last filmed in Blackburn and once completed would be shown in the classroom to the parents and teachers.

This was without doubt the youngest audience I had ever exhibited the films to and the narrative script had to be changed to one of interaction and instruction. The children were asked to clap along to the music, to wave back to the screen when they saw people waving at the camera and to interact with the films on screen. This proved highly successful and Stephen and myself started to respond to what nuances attracted the greatest laughter from the audience in order to be more prepared for the later screenings. The most popular films were the ones featuring children and cheers and booing greeted rival schools captured on screen a century earlier but still relevant to the modern children in the audience.[11] By the end of the day over 800 children had seen the film shows and proved to be an attentive and fascinated audience. Before the afternoon screening the children lined up outside the theatre dressed in their historic costumes with the girls wearing shawls and head scarves and the boys wearing caps and mufflers and paraded down the main road outside the venue, a visual testimony to the continuing power of the local film to amaze, educate and entertain.

Conclusion

This is just an overview of the astonishing journey of the Mitchell & Kenyon local films shows. Later day performances are now held without my input and form part of exhibitions, local history days and screenings. Local films have the power to transform film programming away from the sometimes elite surroundings of the film festival and its cannon. By returning the films back to the locality in which they were taken and empowering the local audience to be part of the show brings us closer to the original purpose that the films were made for. The power of the modern local show reminds us that 'nothing is as good a draw as a local film to bring in an audience'. The Edwardian film exhibitor knew both the power of the local title and the need to advertise this to his audience, more than a century after they were produced, they still retain this same power. Through effective and personalised programming, local marketing and advertising and by involving the audience in the proceedings, the local show continues and remains an essential means of presenting archival material to as wide an audience as possible.

Notes

1. Vanessa Toulmin, Simon Popple and Patrick Russell (eds), *The Lost World of Mitchell & Kenyon: Edwardian Britain on Film* (London: Bfi Publishing, 2004); Vanessa Toulmin, *Electric Edwardians: The Story of the Mitchell & Kenyon Collection* (London: Bfi Publishing, 2006), THE LOST WORLD OF MITCHELL & KENYON, BBC Productions, 2005; DVDs released by the British Film Institute: ELECTRIC EDWARDIANS – THE FILMS OF MITCHELL AND KENYON (2006); MITCHELL AND KENYON IN IRELAND (2007); MITCHELL AND KENYON – EDWARDIAN SPORTS (2007).

2. For more information relating to the public impact of the collection cf. Vanessa Toulmin, "This is a Local Film: The Cultural and Social Impact of the Mitchell & Kenyon Collection" in Jonathan Bate (ed.), *The Public Value of the Humanities* (London: Bloomsbury, 2011), 87–105.

3. Cf. *The Moving Image* 10.1 (2010) on itinerant film making and the local film.

4. Martin Loiperdinger, "'The Audience Feels rather at Home ...' Peter Marzen's 'Localisation' of Film Exhibition in Trier", in Frank Kessler and Nanna Verhoeff (eds), *Networks of Entertainment: Early Film Distribution 1895–1915* (Eastleigh: John Libbey, 2007), 123–130; Uli Jung, "Local Films: A Blind Spot in the Historiography of Early German Cinema", *Historical Journal of Film, Radio and Television*, 22.3 (2003): 253–273; Vanessa Toulmin and Martin Loiperdinger: "Is it You? Representation and Response in Relation to the Local Film", *Film History* 17.1 (2005): 7–19; Martin L. Johnson, "The Places You'll Know: From Self Recognition to Place Recognition in the Local Film", *The Moving Image* 10.1 (2010): 23–50.

5. *The Showman* (30 May 1902): 4.

6. Cf. Toulmin, *Electric Edwardians*.

7. ELECTRIC EDWARDIANS, DVD release.

8. www.cornerhouse.org/film/info.aspx?ID=2307&page=45199, accessed 30 April 2011.

9. For more details of the later show held on 12 and 13 January 2008 see www.admissionall-classes.com/shows_blackpool.php?page=4 including visitor feedback.

10. For more details see www.liv.ac.uk/news/press_releases/2008/04/mitchell-kenyon.htm, accessed 3 March 2010.

11. For the full programme of films presented see www.thwaitesempiretheatre.co.uk/assets/files/Mitchell%20&%20Kenyon%20Programme.pdf, accessed 5 March 2011.

PART II

Crazy Cinématographe
Early Cinema Performance on
the Luxembourg Fairground

Claude Bertemes, Nicole Dahlen

Back to the Future:
Early Cinema and Late Economy of Attention
An interim report about *Crazy Cinématographe*

Devoted to the anonymous spectator who, in the summer of 2009, filled his vomit bag while watching Dr. Doyen's surgical films.

The tumultuous phenomenology of fairgrounds, that sense-numbing simultaneity of flashing lights, candyfloss aroma and screaming roller-coaster riders, is, in a certain respect, like the colourfully iridescent masquerade of a monomaniac functional logic. Fairgrounds, in both historical and contemporary terms, constitute nothing but an unparalleled jostling for attention. The fairground operators, of course, remain subject to the economy of money as ever. However, the surfeit of stimuli in a very enclosed space, which is typical of fairgrounds to an even greater extent than it is of urban environments, turn them into a classic arena and experimental ground for an "economy of attention".[1] If attention is defined as the recipient-side selection of stimuli, it becomes clear why a surplus of attractions and stimuli brings about a relative depletion of the anthropologically limited resource of attention.

The *Crazy Cinématographe project* – in other words, the attempt to revitalise the historic fairground cinema for present-day spectators[2] – is therefore, aside from any nostalgia-fair romanticism, a hazardous venture whose success is a priori improbable. In comparison with the historical fairground cinema, its starting situation from an economy-of-attention point of view is doubly precarious.

It has been pointed out on many occasions that a significant proportion of the thrill of the historical fairground cinema was accounted by the still (technically and socially) emergent medium of film. The new apparatus, and the technical quantum leap which accompanied it, was a potent attention factor compared with the other fairground attractions around the turn of the 20th century (e.g. the menageries, magic shows and theatres of illusion). In terms of content as well, the film pioneers were able to leave the fairgrounds' established live performances trailing – for example with trick film illusions or the realistic

---

Facing page.
Upper: An unparalleled jostling for attention. Picture postcard of a 19th-century German fairground.
Lower: Attracting attention in a modern fairground environment: Schueberfouer 2008.

portrayal of exotica. The auguries for the *Crazy Cinématographe* project, by way of contrast, have been reversed: the intention is for an attraction paradigm more than a hundred years old to prove its worth in a modern fairground environment which involves the experiencing of qualities which are highly tuned-up both technically and sensation-wise.

In addition to this, *Crazy Cinématographe* is aimed at contemporary spectators whose members constitute the very antithesis of the 'Uncle Josh' figure or the Lumière audience which has allegedly been fleeing from the locomotive: late-modern, enlightened media navigators who, after successfully graduating from a "anthropotechnical"[3] training camp in multiplex chairs and in front of digital displays, ought to be largely immunised against the attraction potential of a Méliès-style stop trick.

Against this backdrop, the central challenge for those responsible for *Crazy Cinématographe* has been to develop a genuine audience strategy which can neither restrict itself to historicist reconstruction (where, according to Heraclitus, one cannot step twice into the same river), nor believe, in a helpless gesture, that it can rival the communicative deliria of "mental capitalism" (Georg Franck).

Variatio delectat: (re-)construction of a meandering attention dramaturgy

Crazy Cinématographe is a project of dual incontemporaneity: on the one hand anchored in the late-modern here and now, and on the other referring back to a historical model – the fairground cinema of the *fin-de-siècle* – which for its part is not without ambivalences as regards historical epochs. The new medium of cinematography can at least be placed in a transition period comprising the 19th and 20th centuries which has frequently – from Georg Simmel via Sigmund Freud to Walter Benjamin – been interpreted as the final assertion of the forms of experience and the arousal qualities of the modern age.[4] In our opinion, the hybrid incontemporaneity of *Crazy Cinématographe*, its crossover navigation between the 19th, 20th and 21st centuries, its relaxedly paradoxical epoch changeovers between the proto-modern, modern and late-modern, constitutes the foundation of its singularity and of its success with the public. Below we give a concrete form to this hypothesis using the experience and attention model offered by *Crazy Cinématographe*.

In his last work, *Charles Baudelaire: A Lyric Poet in the Era of High Capitalism*, Walter Benjamin reconstructs the transition to the modern age using the guiding difference 'experiencing' (*Erlebnis*) versus 'experience' (*Erfahrung*), around which, in turn, he organises a richly diverse list of dialectical conceptual dualities, as Susanne Kaufmann emphasises:

> 'Experience' diminishes and 'experiencing' remains, and 'information' takes the place of 'storytelling', while 'aura' disappears to be replaced by 'chock'; the auratically charged work of art is making way for the standard works of art produced using the means of modern reproduction technology, while the leisured

flaneur is being replaced by the anonymous, driven, mass man (...) Here, two seemingly completely different types of language and experience are being confronted with each other; in the process, the former term [i.e. experience] stands for the natural, the continuous, the total, and is confronted with a technical, discontinuous and fragmentary approach [i.e. experiencing].[5]

In relation to early cinema and its audience model, the conceptual duality of experience/experiencing can be differentiated with regard to two fundamental dimensions:

anthropologically speaking, the differentiation between distant experience on the one hand, which guarantees personal integrity and/or individuality, and experiencing-wise proximity, which is accompanied by a direct audience address and "somatisation" of the spectator's gaze,[6] on the other;

structurally speaking, the differentiation between, on the one hand, experience as a mode of continuous and intensive attention, and on the other, experiencing as a fragmented and intermittent attention.

On the basis of this dual binary evolvement of terms, the following four-field matrix of possible attention modes can be drawn up in relation to early cinema:

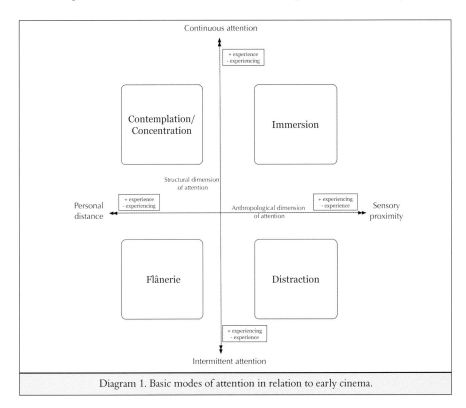

Diagram 1. Basic modes of attention in relation to early cinema.

The attention modes which were presumably most typical of historical fairground cinema are *distraction* and *immersion*. At least both concepts follow on from Benjamin and have been theorised about more than any others within

Rapidly changing scenes and slapstick variations. PREMIÈRE SORTIE D'UNE CYCLISTE, France 1907.

the environment of the 'Cinema of Attractions' discourse.[7] In both cases, to use Benjamin's terms, there is an 'absorption' (*Versenkung*) of the screen stimuli into the spectators' collective body – hence the 'tactile' or somatic nature of the reception. *Immersive* spectator bonding is typically combined with persistently high suggestive force of the screen space which can be attributed to, for example, its kinetic, plastic or sensomotor power of attraction (in the case of phantom rides, for example) or alternatively to the mobilisation of overwhelming 'never been seen' image resources and visual taboos (e.g. in erotic scenes or freak shows). By contrast, *distraction* is structurally and temporally deconstructed, quasi fragmented into disparate attention splinters which change their registers rapidly.[8] The distraction principle is, in a fundamental way, typical of the varied and highly contrasting overall dramaturgy of the historical fairground cinema programmes. Here, however, we are using the term 'distraction' in a more refined way, related to an individual film and interpreted as a possible variable in the attention dramaturgy of a specific film programme. Seen from this viewpoint, certain genres can have a particular affinity for distraction. The burlesque chases genre, for example, seems to be geared primarily towards distraction: its loosely connected station dramaturgy is primarily an excuse for diversified visual pleasure in the form of rapidly changing scenes and slapstick variations.

Under the influence of Benjamin's modernity thesis and his theorisation regarding a somatic-tactile, kaleidoscopic and collectivised reception of film,

Photogénie and auratic dignity. DANSA SERPENTINA, France 1900.

the 'Cinema of Attractions' paradigm has not categorically excluded the possibility of 'pre-modern' modes of experiencing early cinema, although de facto it has hardly taken them into consideration. Even though it seems coherent to attribute a dominant function to the immersive and distractive components in early cinema, we believe that it would be undialectical to underestimate the capacity of spectators in the *Belle Époque* to adopt a personal, self-centred distance from the cinematic apparatus or, in an even more unforced way, simply to uphold it from the outset. The *concentration* mode, for example, in other words the maintenance of a cognitive distance, plays a considerable part in the reception of non-fictional *actualités* and local films.[9] *Contemplation* as a mode of auratically distant[10] concentration is related directly to the concept of *photogénie* in the French theoretical tradition influenced mainly by Jean Epstein and Louis Delluc and can be interpreted as its recipient-side expression. *Photogénie* endows the cinematographically recorded world of things with a generalised auratic dignity which is itself anchored in the cinematographic process: "This process of abstraction, Epstein perceived, endowed objects with an aura of universitality, quintessence, or prototypicality".[11] It can nevertheless be assumed that some genres of fairground cinema, such as coloured serpentine dances or *féeries*, have greater affinity with a contemplative mode than others.

Finally, *flânerie* (strolling) stands for intermittent attention which, in contrast to distraction, encompasses absorption by the world of things rather than the absorption of the world of things into oneself. The perspective of the *flâneur*, according to Harald Neumeyer's analysis of E.T.A. Hoffmann's short story *My Cousin's Corner Window*, requires an "olympian point of view" which always remains aloof.[12] The auctorial mastery of an individualised point of view which indeed does not completely dissolve in a tempest of stimuli therefore marks the categorical boundary between olympian *flânerie* and somatic distraction. It is highly probable that historical fairground cinema *also* had room for a *flâneur* point of view thus defined: for example for the visitor to the cinema tent who was exploring both interestedly and distantly in equal measure and whose gaze and attention wandered between the action on the screen, the pianists, the film narrators and the projecting equipment.[13]

Historical fairground cinema was certainly shaped in a distinctive way by the attention modes of immersion and distraction. The thoughts outlined above in relation to the associated complementary functions of contemplation/concentration and *flânerie*, however, put us in agreement with Singer's nuanced treatment of the modernity thesis:

> Did viewers in 1910 really feel that film images were 'tumbling from fleeting impression to fleeting impression' and 'pass[ing] by at dizzying speeds'? Many early films do not really look and feel that way. (...) Let us accept, for the sake of argument, that a contemporary viewer asked to sit through a program of *typical* early films (not just films selected to support a hyperdynamic characterization) normally would find them less astonishing, less charged with powerful attraction, less viscerally arousing, less kaleidoscopic and 'phantasmagoric' than (...) proponents of the modernity thesis would lead one to assume was the norm a century ago.[14]

As will be demonstrated in the following case studies, the programming and presentation strategy of *Crazy Cinématographe* is aimed at a seemingly effortlessly wandering[15] attention dramaturgy which meanders between the poles of immersion, distraction, contemplation/concentration and *flânerie*. Even though the specific means applied are adjusted to late-modern experience horizons on a case-by-case basis, the resultant experience structure is similar to that of historical fairground cinema both structurally and functionally. The fluid change between the attention modes in which the entertainment principle 'variatio delectat' articulates itself is achieved not only with the composition of the film programme, but also additionally by the construction of a theatricalised overall dramaturgy. This *'performative turn'*, which the *Crazy Cinématographe* project practically reproduces (via integration of front shows, film narrators, sound effect men, etc.), is likely to have been discussed in fundamental terms in the theory of early cinema but has hardly been put into practice in individual case analyses. The following case studies attempt to enter this *terra incognita*.

(Re-)construction of the historical: the curatorial guidelines

The major challenge for the curators of the *Crazy Cinématographe* programmes (Nicole Dahlen, Claude Bertemes and, in 2007, Vanessa Toulmin)[16] has been first of all to gear the prospection and selection of historical fairground films

Bizarre 'excavation' from the interior of the human body. CHEZ LE DENTISTE (France 1907).

towards the central idea that the selected films *as such* can arouse the attention of a present-day audience – i.e. have an inherent attention potential. In addition, it has been necessary as a second step to model the selected body of films into attractive programme concepts and dramaturgies, with considerations of this kind exerting a retrospective influence on the selection procedure.

To evaluate the attention value of the pre-viewed films, the curators took on the role of an ideal-typical test audience of the late-modern period, so to speak, by taking off their film-history spectacles and instead trying to display a kind of second-degree naiveté.[17] In this way, the special aura that the scientific community attributes to some films solely on the basis of canonisation on film history or film studies grounds is deliberately excluded as a criterion for selection. In exceptional cases where film-historical reflexes have been able to assert themselves, the academic expertise was corrected, at the latest, in the light of audience expertise. One example of this, as incisive as it is sobering, is the *Crazy Pot-Pourri* module that was presented at the Luxembourgian fairground *Schueberfouer* in 2009. The decision to include Louis Lumière's emblematic sketch ARROSEUR ET ARROSÉ in the programme was based on, among other things, the didactic élan for communicating to spectators the historical significance of this first film burlesque. After the first showings, however, it became evident that this film considerably impaired the spectators' consistency of attention (and therefore the module's rhythm), with the result that it had to be removed from the programme. Faulty evaluations of this kind can generally be prevented beforehand in the pre-test phase, in this case the trial runs with the film narrators lasting several days. During these tests, two different perspectives intersected and corrected one another: that of the film narrators and that of the film curators. In both cases, the viewpoint in question was hardly clouded by film-historical filters: the professional expertise of the *Compagnie des Bonimenteurs* is a priori not based on knowledge of film history, while the film curators in the test situation found themselves for the first time confronted not with a historical corpus of films but with a theatricalised live spectacle. In this way, the film curators' point of view has shifted substantially: from the insider perspective of selecting and programming historical films to an external view of their own programme work, which henceforth the curators encountered as an 'objectified' product, so to speak.

Even though the project's basic approach is historically motivated – namely to revive the fairground cinema of the 1900s –, the curatorial strategy thereby, for the aforementioned reasons, extracts itself from the straitjacket of historicism in a number of respects and to some extent in significant ways:

The basic components of the *Crazy Cinématographe* apparatus correspond to those of historical fairground cinema: the showings in a cinema tent amidst the competing environment of a fairground's attractions; the films being aimed at a socially heterogeneous audience; the blatant 'parade' of the barkers outside the front area; the sometimes soberly explanatory, sometimes contrapuntally jocular, sometimes dramatically inflammatory comments in the film programmes by the film narrators and the use of sound effect men. The *Crazy Cinématographe* showings are each accompanied live by a pianist, although it has not been established for sure whether and, if so, to what extent piano accompaniment was part of the historical apparatus. The film projector, as an eye-catcher, is in the auditorium, which corresponds to historical practice until 1900.[18] If the details are examined, however, there are numerous deviations from the historical model: the *Crazy Cinématographe* tent has room for 120 people, while historical tent-cinema operators had much larger capacities – up to 2,000 seats. All in all, *Crazy Cinématographe* is probably a hybrid form located between the small cinematograph booths fashioned out of wood and the mobile 'electric fairytale palaces' flaunting their ornamental tent exteriors. An electric cinema organ is lacking in the *Crazy Cinématographe* apparatus, as are the 'locomobiles' (mobile engines for generating power) and the operation of the projector using a crank handle.[19]

The programme being staged by *Crazy Cinématographe* consists, in line with the historical model, of varied short film programmes (*Nummernprogramme*) of some 20 minutes' duration which generally comprise 6 to a maximum of 12 films. In a divergence from the historical tradition, however, *Crazy Cinématographe* does not restrict itself to the programme forms of the general, thematically mixed showing (*Crazy Pot-Pourri*) and the special showing for adults (*Erotique 1900*). As part of the strategy of developing accentuated identities for specific show modules and thereby of intensifying the appeal to the public, the curators also conceived thematically-oriented modules: a comedy module

Sometimes soberly explanatory, sometimes contrapuntally jocular, sometimes dramatically inflammatory comments. The *Crazy Cinématographe* Apparatus (interior), Schueberfouer 2008.

(*Comedy & Burlesque*), a *féerie* and trick film module (*Magical Mystery Tour*), a module with freaks (*Cabinet of the Bizarre*), an animal film module (*Cabinet of Crazy Animals*), an operation film module (*Dr. Doyen's Surgical Cabinet*), an artists' and variety module (*Cabinet Fantastico*) and thematic *special events*.[20]

In a manner similar to that of historical fairground cinema, the entire spectrum of the genres in early cinema is not depicted in a representative way in the *Crazy Cinématographe* programme. The genres in the fictional segment favoured by the curators are comedies, *féeries* and trick films, and erotic scenes, while melodramas, theatrical scenes and historical films are under-represented. Dramas and films inspired by the theatrical canon or ancient mythology generally have the disadvantage that they are longer than 4 to 5 minutes and therefore exceed the dramaturgical limit of a maximum 20-minute programme length. In addition, they often suffer from what, for present-day viewing habits, is an artificial dramaturgy and a sometimes embarrassing pathos – both are potentially distancing, attention-reducing factors. With regard to the historical films of early cinema, moreover, there is the problem of dual historical distance. Today, these films have become historical in their own right and must therefore be deciphered doubly, with neither the cultural codes of the narrated myth itself nor – and this is the more serious point – those of its reinterpretation in the *Belle Époque* likely to be familiar to present-day spectators. The dominance of particular fictional genres practised in *Crazy Cinématographe*, however, is probably a rough approximation of the historical reality of fairground cinema in which, according to Garncarz, "fairy plays on the one hand and situation comedies on the other"[21] were predominant.

As far as the non-fictional genres are concerned, the dominant elements are artists', variety and magic acts on the one hand, and those scientific and/or nature films which, whether intentionally or unintentionally, explore the realm of the sensational, the thrilling or the taboo, on the other.[22] Local film material was integrated selectively into the mixed *Crazy Pot-Pourri* modules. In contrast to historical fairground cinema, *actualités* and exotic travelogues were not included in the programme because it can be assumed that their experience value and visual appeal are hardly likely to have outlasted the historical passage of time.

Case study 1: *Crazy Pot-Pourri*, Schueberfouer 2008

Compared with the thematic modules, the *Crazy Pot-Pourri* concept is oriented most genuinely towards the historical central idea of genre diversity and the programme of short items rich in contrasts. This was also the case with *Crazy Pot-Pourri*, which was presented at the *Schueberfouer* in Luxembourg in 2008: a graceful serpentine dance was followed by a parodic animal number, a playful *féerie* by a racy animated film, and a vaudeville act by a local film. Specifically, the *Crazy Pot-Pourri* 2008 module consists of the following show elements or films:

1. *Front show* (approx. 15 minutes): Two barkers attired in belle epoque style each stand on the stage outside the front area before the programme begins and try to attract the attention of members of the public as they pass by. They tout the sensations and diversity of the *Crazy Pot-Pourri* programme and promise an unbelievable journey into "cinema's crazy childhood". Some passers-by remain standing, in the process discovering the cinema tent, follow the front show with one ear, cast a glance at the programme placard or let themselves be drawn into a conversation with the students who are distributing leaflets in front of the stage. The walk to the box office, should it ensue, is described as exemplary by the barkers. All in all, the interested elements of the public are characterised primarily by lethargic, remote attention which wanders between the front show, the ice-cream cones in their hands and the mewling children in tow.

2. *The spectators take their seats* (approx. 5 minutes): After having their tickets checked, the spectators enter the cinema tent and take a seat on one of the wooden benches. While the barkers in front of the tent continue their efforts to fill the rows for a few more minutes, it is time for the spectator to let his eyes wander. He has been promised a journey into the past, but gets the impression that in certain respects he is entering new territory. Perhaps he will see things that have never been seen before and hear unheard-of things. On the front wall he notices the red velour curtains, which possibly remind him of a David Lynch film and fortify his impression that he has ended up in a peculiar puzzle. At the front on the right, a man aged about 55 sits down at the piano. He has very grey, slightly tousled hair and is wearing an old-fashioned waistcoat and round spectacles with metal frames. The pianist seems like a throwback to an earlier era, yet the fresh draught beer that he is now putting down on the wooden floor next to the piano is in a plastic mug. The spectator's gaze wanders to the screen: it is pretty imposing, has art nouveau-style rolling contours and ornaments and is, curiously, made from white-painted wood. On the left, next to the screen, there are various small instruments on a repository. The spectator now turns his head to get a closer look

at the projector that he had noticed as soon as he entered the tent. A majestic institution, an expression of powerful, cast-steel mechanics. He cannot remember having seen anything like it before. Then the film narrators enter the tent – now it's time to pay attention!

3. *Introduction* (approx. 5 minutes): The two film narrators introduce themselves to the audience as the siblings Vincent and Marie Minestrone. They say that they appeared in New York the day before in front of 100,000 people, when the women enthusiastically threw their brassieres, and the men their wives, onto the stage in Vincent's direction. They therefore see themselves as being entitled to demand thunderous applause, which the audience then provides – but not without a hint of expectant reticence. In a ping-pong exchange, Vincent and Marie recount the bafflingly distant years of the films' production, from 1897 to 1909, the various countries in which they were produced, from France to Poland, and the genres to be anticipated, from the animated film to the documentary scene. Then, fictitious safety measures in the event of anticipated gales of laughter are practiced together with the audience. With a fulsome gesture, Vincent then gives the projectionist the starting signal and invites the public to pay close attention to the purring rumble of the projector. Most of the spectators turn their heads towards the projector while its light cone shines and is cast onto the screen over the heads of the audience.

4. DANSE SERPENTINE [II] (France c1897, Lumière, 1 minute, hand-coloured): In the restaging of Loïe Fuller's serpentine dance, the female dancer, who remains anonymous, moves on a light brown wooden stage in front of black curtains. In comparison with the nymph-like, improvising Annabelle Moore in the Edison films, the dancing performance seems more professional and closer to Loïe Fuller's ideal. The very eye-catching, rather crude wooden stage provides a naturalistic contrast to the delicate hand-coloured veil's movements. The film narrators switch between a didactic register, which explains the historical background, and an admirative register which emphasises the scene's gracefulness.

5. CHIENS SAVANTS: LA DANSE SERPENTINE (France 1898, Lumière, 1 minute): A dog trainer leads a poodle standing on its hind legs onto the scene; the poodle is dressed with a flapping white cape, long leggings and a hat adorned with a girdle of flowers. The erect poodle makes circling movements which are clearly a parody of snake dances. Its eyes regularly turn to the left-hand edge of the screen, where the dog trainer can sometimes partly be seen before disappearing off-screen again. In the background, six dogs of different breeds are sitting on pedestals placed in a row. They do not even deign to look at the dancing dog, however, instead directing their gaze pointedly towards the left-hand edge of the screen. At the end of the film, the clearly exhausted poodle collapses into the left-hand off-screen area. The film narrators' commentary is reserved, although it does refer to the dog's increasing tiredness.

6. UPSIDE DOWN, OR: THE HUMAN FLIES (GB 1899, Paul's Animatograph Works, 1 minute): A magician enters a salon where he is received by a solid, diligent middle-class family and he proceeds to gradually suspend the laws of gravity: he picks up a table with an outstretched hand, makes his top hat ascend into the air and finally raises the residents to just below the ceiling, where they remain fixed upside-down like flies. The family members test the spatial coordinates of their out-of-joint new existence by hopping around in a carefree manner. The film narrators' commentary is reserved, largely leaving the suggestive power of the spatial illusion to the audience.

Old-fashioned waistcoast and round spectacles. Pianist Philippe, Schueberfouer 2008.

7. L'HOMME QUI MARCHE SUR LA TÊTE (France 1909, Pathé, 4 minutes, tinted): In front of a palatial backdrop, Monsieur Tack presents several acrobatic numbers, all of which he completes 'head over heels' at an ascending level of difficulty: he takes off his tuxedo, balances rotating on one arm, jumps rope and climbs up the stairs. The film narrators dramatise the physical dangers of the numbers, warn the spectators and make reference to headaches, brain damage and fractures. During the rope jumping and stair climbing, the sound effect men accompany every bump of the head with crashing percussion sounds.

8. LA PEINE DU TALION (France 1906, Pathé, 5 minutes, stencil-coloured): In this *féerie*, a distinguished butterfly collector goes hunting with his two female assistants against a woodland backdrop. The woods are inhabited by larger-than-life butterflies – in the form of flightily dancing actresses in elaborately coloured costumes. The butterflies transform the assistants into locusts and quote the collector before a butterfly court, which sentences him to endure the fate of a butterfly and be skewered on an enormous cork. Everything blows over with the closing apotheosis typical of the genre. The film narrators comment on the film's narrative line on the one hand, but refer repeatedly to the charming poetry of the genre and the ancient technique of stencil colouring.

9. THÉÂTRE DE HULA HULA (not identified, 1 minute): In this early animated film, dated to 1917 by some sources, a four-piece jazz combo strikes up in the forefront of the picture. Its members are wearing nothing but Hawaiian hula skirts. The curtain, on which "Théâtre de Hula Hula" can be read, rises to reveal a South Seas backdrop, implied by two coconut trees, in which a female dancer with pinned-up hairdo does a hula parody. A male surfer, short of stature, joins her, and the floundering dance performance is increasingly determined by grotesque, rubbery physical deformations and transformations. The film narrators restrict themselves

ATHLETE RUPPRECHT. Fragment of a Polish actualité, Poland c1910.

mainly to egging on the audience, while the pianist and the sound effect men crank up the atmosphere with gusto.

10. [ATHLETE RUPPRECHT] (Poland c1910, Odeon Czestochowa, 1 minute): This is a fragment of a Polish *actualité* dedicated to the Victoria sports club. The fragment shows the strongman Rupprecht, firstly in a frontal medium shot and then while executing three tests of strength. First of all, the athlete performs a one-armed pull-up with lead balls attached to his legs, then he drives steel nails into a wooden board with his bare hands, and finally he is stretched between two horses with leather belts and brings them to a standstill. The fragment is punctuated by historical title cards with Polish explanatory texts and art-nouveau borders. The comments by the film narrators give ironic treatment to the phenomenon of the strongman and underline the incomprehensibility of the intertitles.

11. PREMIÈRE SORTIE D'UNE CYCLISTE (France 1907, Pathé, 5 minutes): A young woman dressed in white goes out for a ride on her newly-acquired bicycle for the first time. In doing so, she systematically collides with all the people, animals and objects that cross her path: a baby's pram, a horse-drawn carriage, a group of picnickers, a herd of sheep and an exercising military group. Although the cyclist is chased only by the group of soldiers, the film varies the dramaturgical principle of chase films: the succession of burlesque mishaps. The sound effect men mark every collision with bicycle bells and drumbeats, thereby underlining the comical ostinato of the heralded catastrophes.

12. LES SIX SŒURS DAINEF (France 1902, Pathé, 4 minutes, hand-coloured): Six sisters, some of them plump, present lively acrobatic numbers on a stage covered by an extensive carpet in front of an ornamental backdrop which provides a perspective view over an external entrance and a park landscape. The programme contains rapidly changing stunts encompassing a rotating human pyramid, rapid back-handspring and salto numbers and ultimately bizarre, beetle-like two- and three-person formations. The film narrators stoke up the dynamism of the scenes and bring the audience into the action by encouraging them to count the saltos which ensue in rapid succession.

13. SUR LES REMPARTS DE LUXEMBOURG (France c1919, Pathé Revue, 1 minute, stencil-coloured): This cultural education film from the Pathé Revue collection shows picturesque, mostly deserted panorama shots of the city of Luxemburg. The film is a recent archival discovery and was shown again for the first time at the Schueberfouer in 2008. The historical significance of this finding was underlined by the fact that the film, stencil-coloured using the *Pathécolor* process, is the earliest colour film about Luxembourg still in existence. Although the touristy postcard-like aesthetics differ markedly from those of the local films genre, the film de facto assumes the local-film "identifying recognition" function when shown at a Luxembourg fairground. The film ends with a bucolic view of the Alzette river landscape. The film narrators comment on the film in a discreet fashion.

14. BONSOIR [TABLEAU FLEURI] (France 1906, Gaumont, 1 minute, stencil-coloured): Two young women in medieval knaves' costume empty two baskets of flower blossoms on to a table on which a large board is standing. As if by magic, the blossoms fall into place on the board to form the lettering "Bonsoir". The young women bid farewell by blowing kisses to the audience. The film belongs to the specific genre of the *bonsoir* films in early cinema with their 'chucking-out' function. The film narrators announce the end of the show.

15. *The spectators leave the tent:* While the auditorium lights are switched on again, the film narrators thank the audience, the pianists and the projectionists. They refer the audience to the subsequent programme modules, in particular the erotic shows from 10 pm onwards for an adult audience. Then they dance to an improvisation by the pianist while the spectators leave the tent at a relaxed, sauntering pace. Most of the audience benefit from letting their eyes wander once again, as though this would help to improve their understanding of what they had experienced. Some spectators remain there for a while in order to talk to the film narrators, the pianist or the projectionist, while others inspect the instrument box or the projector. The most courageous ones venture to take a look behind the scenes, behind the Lynch-like red curtains.

The above description of the fifteen different show elements is intended to demonstrate in specific detail how and with what curational selection, pro-gramme-structural and theatrical performance strategies the *Crazy Pot-Pourri* module puts the basic dramaturgical principle of *variety* into practice – a principle which is generally constitutive for historical fairground cinema. In our opinion, the genre diversity which is often quoted in accounts of film history describes variety only in an extrinsic, supply-oriented and schematising way.[23] If the phenomenon of variety is to be recorded in a more genuine and differentiated way, it requires an audience- and experiencing-oriented explanatory model which, in addition, includes the performative (or 'theatrical') dimension of fairground cinema in the analysis.

In our opinion, the variety principle as achieved in the *Crazy Pot-Pourri* module is ultimately attributable to a lasting change in the how different attention modes are experienced, as a result of which an entanglement of concentrated, wandering, distractive and immersive viewing became possible. In Diagram 2, the dramaturgical line of the *Crazy Pot-Pourri* module is depicted as a projection of its 15 consecutive elements onto the matrix of different attention modes (Diagram 1) which is discussed theoretically above. The methodical basis for the respective positioning of the 15 elements on the matrix was not the curators' original calculation during the programme conception work, but the – in an empirical sense – participatory observation by the curators, who regularly mingled with the audience at the *Schueberfouer*.[24]

To help you understand the matrix better, we would like to formulate short hypotheses by using selected show elements in relation to their respective attention coordinates:[25]

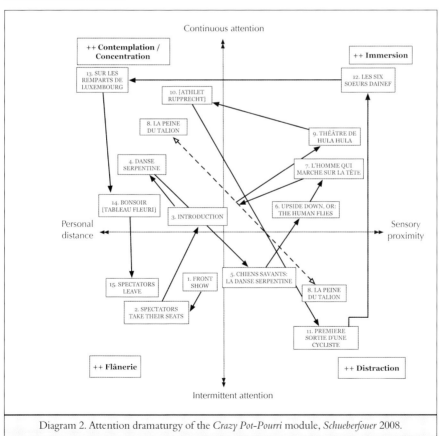

Diagram 2. Attention dramaturgy of the *Crazy Pot-Pourri* module, *Schueberfouer* 2008.

Front Show (#1): The spectators who remain standing are in close proximity to a theatrical spectacle but still take care to maintain the necessary distance. Their attention is by no means focused entirely on the front show by the barkers; it is split, still dominated by the habitus of the strolling passers-by among whose number they had been just a few moments before.

The spectators take their seats (#2): The basic attitude of the spectators awaiting the action in the tent is one of relaxed exploration. Their viewing is unfocused and wandering on the one hand, and characterised by a high level of spectatorial autonomy on the other, a result of their relatively shielded situation.

Introduction (#3): When the actual show begins, the spectators' concentration intensifies. Only with hesitation, however, do they yield to the sensory tumult that the film narrators strive to unleash with their warm-up programme.[26]

Danse Serpentine (#4): The spectators attentively follow a film whose genre they were hitherto unaware of and whose colouring both surprises them and puts them in a contemplative mood. The naturalistic stage creates distance and the spectator's gaze does not immerse itself in the scene.[27]

Chiens savants (#5): The spectators focus only to a limited extent on the poodle dancing in the centre of the picture, because they are permanently distracted by the happenings on the left-hand edge of the screen and by the lined-up dogs in the background. The circus-like atmosphere and certain movement dynamics create a limited degree of sensory proximity.

La Peine du talion (#8): The film provokes two diametrically different attention modes between which the spectator oscillates to and fro. On the one hand, the genre of the coloured *féeries* invites spectators to adopt a contemplative basic attitude. On the other, La Peine du talion is distinguished by a narrative zigzag course which is distractive in a positively flighty way: when, for example, the two young assistants suddenly change into enormous hopping locusts which, for their part, later mutate – for unfathomable reasons – into wardresses of the butterfly kingdom.

Athlete Rupprecht (#10): The combination of documentary form and spectacular content trigger concentrated attention. The Polish intertitles and the sober pointing gesture create distance and block the immersive effect that sometimes characterises artists' numbers.

Première sortie d'une cycliste (#11): The fast-paced variation of a burlesque leitmotif is highly entertaining. The episodic narrative arc enables spectators to show intermittent attention in an ideal way while simultaneously being exposed to a permanent wake-up call from sensory effects – spectacular collisions accentuated by bicycle bells, drum rolls and drumbeats.

Sur les remparts de Luxembourg (#13): The film narrators have told the audience of the historical significance of this archive discovery for Luxembourg, and at the same time the city's pastel colouring and deserted condition lend its images an auratic abstraction. The film provokes a very high level of concentration, coupled with contemplative distance.

If we look at the matrix in its entirety, the principle of meandering attention dramaturgy is immediately palpable: to use a simple set phrase, it expresses itself in the dramaturgical line's zigzag course. In the overwhelming majority of cases – to be precise, in 11 of 14 cases – the transition from one show module to the next is connected with a switch from one of the four matrix fields (i.e. attention modes) to another. In particular cases, the dramaturgy is geared

High indexality of the attractions shown. L'HOMME QUI MARCHE SUR LA TÊTE, France 1909.

towards sometimes spectacular 'emotional roller coasters', as e.g. the hiatus between ATHLETE RUPPRECHT (high concentration) and PREMIÈRE SORTIE D'UNE CYCLISTE (maximum distraction) or the jump from LES SIX SŒURS DAINEF (maximum immersion) to SUR LES REMPARTS DE LUXEMBOURG (maximum contemplation) suggest. It is also striking that the weighting between the four attention fields is reasonably balanced, although this is qualified by the fact that the *flânerie* mode applies only with reference to the enframing show elements (and not to the film programme).

In addition to variety, *heightening* is the second basic principle of the dramaturgy of early cinema.[28] Irrespective of the high base level of excitement which, in line with the 'Cinema of Attractions' paradigm, can be assumed in fairground cinema, this must be modulated if it is to have an entertaining effect. Or, to use the converse argument, bombarding the audience permanently with stimuli at the highest excitement level would quickly cause those watching to switch off. In Diagram 2 it can be seen how the dramaturgical narrative arc gradually intensifies till, shortly before the module comes to an end, it achieves the maximum levels of immersion (LES SIX SŒURS DAINEF) and concentration/contemplation (SUR LES REMPARTS DE LUXEMBOURG). This is followed by a rapid flattening of the attention curve with the film BONSOIR and the departure of the audience.

The principle of progressive heightening can not only be comprehended on the basis of the module's overall dramaturgy; it also repeats itself significantly in the four different attention fields. The crescendo of the immersion-oriented films, from UPSIDE DOWN through L'HOMME QUI MARCHE SUR LA TÊTE and THÉÂTRE DE HULA HULA to LES SIX SŒURS DAINEF, makes a particularly strong impression. The immersive strategy of UPSIDE DOWN is to invite spectators to plunge themselves into an illusionist space and participate in its inverted gravitation logic. Michael Brooke has pointed out that the director W.R. Booth invented the technical trick of camera rotation for this, the trick that Stanley Kubrick used 70 years later in similar but refined form in his highly immersive masterpiece 2001: A SPACE ODYSSEY (1968).[29] The immersion effect of UPSIDE DOWN is limited, however, because the trick technique is used in a rather rudimentary way[30] and, in addition, strong habituation effects can be expected from late-modern audiences especially in relation to spectacular spatial illusions, which are among the most consistently practiced immersion strategies of blockbuster cinema.

L'HOMME QUI MARCHE SUR LA TÊTE is a direct echo of UPSIDE DOWN's 'topsy-turvy world' motif. Compared with Booth's film, its immersive potential presumably derives from the fact that it is noticeably *not* an animated film, i.e. in the high indexality of the attractions shown. This ought to be a rather surprising cinema experience for latter-day audiences conditioned to virtual realities: *reality bites*, so to speak. The immersive effect is therefore somewhat stronger. At the same time, L'HOMME QUI MARCHE SUR LA TÊTE articulates a different immersive *quality* from UPSIDE DOWN – to use the term coined for contemporary blockbuster cinema by Robin Curtis and Christiane Voss, its immersive effects "jump upon" rather than "pull in":

> The theatrical presentation form and effect, then, is present in the direct addressing method, and therefore aims for spectacle and loud attention. Here, the spectator is not pulled into an event being staged; on the contrary, he is genuinely jumped upon by that event, for example by means of a motif, sound or colour effect coming towards him. While Fried does not treat the theatrically generated effects as forms of immersion, it can nevertheless be concluded that while image effects which jump upon their recipients may reverse the direction of the entanglement, they can still be called immersive provided that they entangle him by means of an appeal or surprise attack. The shock effects, special effects and wild image and sound montages of many blockbuster films aim for surprise attacks and provide examples of immersive effects resulting from aggressive theatricality.[31]

Generally speaking, the 'jumping-upon' type of immersion in the cinema of attractions occurs more frequently than 'pulling-in' immersion. "Aggressive theatricality" is a genuine hallmark of early cinema which can be regarded at least as much as a late-theatrical form of 19th-century popular culture than as an early cinematographic form of 20th-century media-related modernity. Both THÉÂTRE DE HULA HULA and LES SIX SŒURS DAINEF are prime examples of jumping-upon theatricality: they develop their suggestive power by staging ecstatic bodies which are accelerated, choreographed and modulated above and beyond the laws of everyday physics. In the process, the furious dynamism of the endlessly whirling Dainef sisters, in turn, has the immersive advantage of greater indexality compared with the bodily deformations animated in the hula-hula theatre.[32] Apart from that, the *mise en scène* of LES SIX SŒURS DAINEF deliberately divides the room into the stage foreground and background, which at times are being performed on simultaneously by the acrobats. Complemented by the *trompe l'œil* view in the background, it thereby develops into not inconsiderable space dynamics and depth, which in turn should facilitate not only jumping-upon but also pulling-in immersion, even if only as a secondary function. Finally, the fact that film narrators, sound effect men and the pianist 'crank it up', to the maximum extent possible, for the purpose of lending additional dynamism to the film's inherent immersion effects should not be underestimated.

Case study 2: *Dr Doyen's Surgical Cabinet, Schueberfouer* 2009

Despite concentrating on a particular genre or subject, the thematic modules of *Crazy Cinématographe* are geared towards entertaining the spectators in a variety of ways. Particular attention is paid to achieving a varied programme rich in contrasts and the greatest possible variance within a genre specification.[33] The attention dramaturgy is basically similar to that in *Crazy Pot-Pourri*.

The *Dr Doyen's Surgical Cabinet* module is a special case; it was presented at the *Schueberfouer* in 2009 and caused a furore both for the audience and in the media reviews and reports. Its success was anything but pre-ordained, though, as the source material, the body of surgical films made by the French surgeon Eugène-Louis Doyen,[34] at first confronted the curators with a quite insoluble paradox. On the one hand, there is historical evidence that the Doyen films were presented at the *Schueberfouer* in Luxembourg in the 1900s as "separate showings" like the erotic stag programmes. An advertisement by Theodor Bläser's *Original-Biograph* in the *Luxemburger Zeitung* dated 25 August 1902 announces the Doyen films as follows: "Schobermesse – Luxemburg. Bläser's Original-Biograph! (...) 9 p.m. every evening: gentlemen's show. Admission only for gentlemen aged 20 or over. (Female doctors can be admitted if accompanied by a gentleman). Operations by the famous surgeon Professor Dr S. Doyen in Paris will be shown." On the other hand, the Doyen films contain visual taboos with an extreme impact, for example the cutting open of a cranium or the removal of monstrously huge tumours. The curators had to assume that the shock effect on a present-day *Schueberfouer* audience (compared with past audiences) would be even greater and that the limits of tolerability would be exceeded. This results in particular from the historical remoteness of the material – the patina of the material, the old-fashioned habitus of Doyen and his assistants, the robust-seeming operation choreography and a number of irritating details[35] – which connote what modern eyes would regard as barbarism from before the dawn of civilisation and slasher-film aesthetics, although at the beginning of the 20th century the Doyen films were designed to document the very *progress* of surgical techniques. In addition, the coordinates of political correctness established in the 21st century are making the blatant exhibiting of such material at fairgrounds more difficult.

Each member of the audience is handed a vomit bag. *Dr Doyen's Surgical Cabinet*, Schueberfouer 2009

The curatorial challenge, then, was to integrate the extreme immersion effects that the Doyen films were assumed to contain into an overall dramaturgy which has a relieving effect both psychologically and politically. The crucial way of solution involved counterpointing bloodthirsty horror films with comical scenes, inspired by the strategy of the French *Grand Guignol* theatre

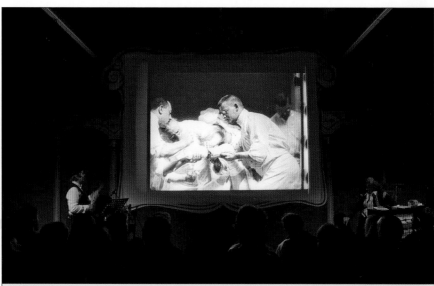

Horror not (yet) shown to its fullest extent. UNTERSCHENKELAMPUTATION (Germany c1903).

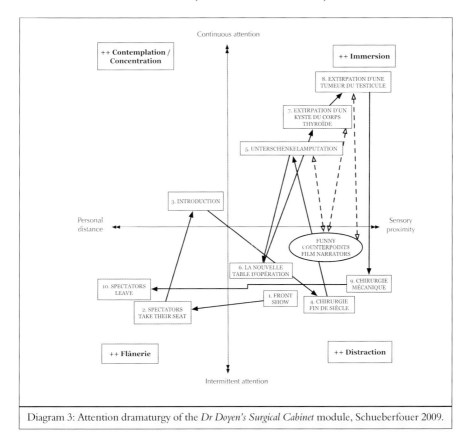

Diagram 3: Attention dramaturgy of the *Dr Doyen's Surgical Cabinet* module, Schueberfouer 2009.

towards the end of the 19th century. Accordingly, the construction of the *Doyen* module was oriented towards the central idea of provoking a dramaturgical oscillation between the attention modes of shock-like immersion and burlesque distraction – in other words, an emotional rollercoaster (cf. Diagram 3).

The oscillation expresses itself either *consecutively*, with the real operation films having been mixed with burlesque Doyen parodies (the films CHIRURGIEN FIN DE SIÈCLE and CHIRURGIE MÉCANIQUE and the heavily theatricalised front show), or *simultaneously* (dashed lines in Diagram 3), with the film narrators resolutely counterpointing the three real operation films with burlesque role patterns.

Even the front show, compared with that of the *Crazy Pot-Pourri* module analysed above, is an entertaining spectacle in its own right: a hyped-up gore film pastiche in which the barkers, dressed in scrubs and a mask, swing disproportionately large saws made from cardboard as they follow the screeching fairground passers-by and then finally, back on the stage, they amputate a lower leg with imitation blood squirting out. Having been introduced, the comical note is sustained for the time being: on entering the tent, each member of the audience is handed a vomit bag, and in their introduction the film narrators make the audience rehearse throwing up into the bag "instead of into your neighbour's lap". The first film, the Pathé production CHIRURGIEN FIN DE SIÈCLE, is a Doyen parody in which the surgeon and his two assistants amputate the patient's right lower arm and lower leg with scissors, a saw and a stop trick carried out in a rudimentary way, in order – again by using an approximate stop trick – to glue on limbs from the spare parts stockroom.

The subsequent film UNTERSCHENKELAMPUTATION provides a shocking contrast to this: it is the first German surgical film, made in 1903, in which the renowned war surgeon Professor Ernst von Bergmann carries out a lower leg amputation in the Berlin Surgical University Clinic – with an amputation knife and a saw, but this time in reality and without a stop trick.[36] Although the surgical choreography is characterised by brute violence, as shown by the spirited application of the saw, the horror is not (yet) shown to its fullest extent: the patient can hardly be seen, with only the left upper leg and buttock not being covered or not being distorted in their appearance by the large surgical team (Bergmann, three assistants and two surgical nurses).[37] The film narrators compensate for the horrors with their ironic comments on the German surgeon's no-nonsense robustness: they present him as the former car mechanic "Doktor von Opel" and enrich his surgical instructions with the appropriate metaphors.[38] The sound effect men accompany the operation with sawing effects.

This is followed by LA NOUVELLE TABLE D'OPÉRATION, a short documentary scene in which Doyen presents the operating table that he had invented – the "Doyen bed". To a present-day audience, the film as such seems unintentionally comical: the demonstration object lying motionless on the Doyen bed is a naked (apart from black stockings) woman's body which Doyen shifts into sometimes grotesque positions by fiddling with his invention and cranking it up and down.[39] The film narrators parody the film's promotional demeanour by praising the operating table's advantages and its unbeatable price in the style of a shopping show on TV.

The two subsequent Doyen films put everything that went before in the shade: their immersive shock effect is so pronounced that the audience reacts with hysterically braying cries as if it were on a rollercoaster ride. In EXTIRPATION D'UN KYSTE DU CORPS THYROÏDE, Doyen makes a cut in the patient's throat area, removes a thyroid cyst the size of a melon, and makes the latter burst open by stabbing it resolutely with a pair of scissors. As a result of this, blood sprays in a long arc onto the white sheet which is scantily covering the male patient. In EXTIRPATION D'UNE TUMEUR DU TESTICULE, Doyen opens up the patient's testicles, from which he pulls out a whitish tumour the size of an orange. The tumour, which is attached to the testicles in the manner of an umbilical cord, is bound and cut off with scissors.

In view of this visual paroxysm, a scenario allocating a decidedly interventionist role for the film narrators was developed as a counterpoint for these two films.[40] The scenario provides for a female and a male part for the Doyen module. The

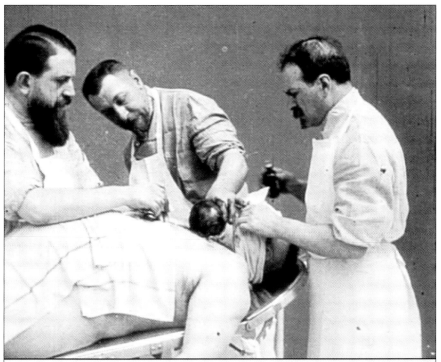

A thyroid cyst the size of a melon. EXTIRPATION D'UN KYSTE DU CORPS THYROÏDE, France 1898/1903.

female part admires Dr Doyen's dexterity and speed[41] and the unparalleled size and beauty of the tumours. In addition, in a sober flow of scientific analysis, she describes the individual surgical steps in detail.[42] By way of contrast, the male film narrator uses comical exaggeration to play the utterly nauseated observer who, out of sheer revulsion, can no longer bear to watch what is going on and, in a panic-stricken crescendo, runs up and down between the rows of spectators. The Dante-like aesthetics of revulsion that the Doyen films convey cannot be neutralised by the film narrators. It was possible, however, to transport them into a double-bind situation of sheer disgust and liberating laughter.

★ ★ ★

Crazy Cinématographe, we would like to conclude, offers the almost singular experiencing of multi-dimensional, elastic attention, in contrast to the media offerings that are dominant in the late-modern period, which are generally geared towards one-dimensional formats. The generalised language of *You-Tube*, *Facebook* and *Twitter* is fragmented distraction; that of the multiplex cinemas alternates between immersion and distraction, mostly enclosed within highly formatted genres, while Hollywood, as a reaction to home cinema, is currently concerned above all with enhancing the immersion spiral of 3D technology. Concentration is increasingly becoming the niche experience of those of us who read – provided that reading still takes place in the linear mode of the printed Gutenberg age and not in the wiping *Flipboard* mode of an *iPad tablet*. The market niche of contemplation is occupied by the resourceful producers of the *FM3 Bouddha Machine*, a low-tech variant of the transistor radios made from transparent plastic that can effect nothing apart from an ambient sound loop. *Flânerie* as a media experience perhaps still exists while browsing through a *Manufactum* catalogue, but apart from that it has virtually died out.

By way of contrast, *Crazy Cinématographe* organises a meandering form of attention, even in its most pointed programmes such as the *Doyen* module. Its language is *heteroglossia* (Mikhail Bakhtin) – the polyphony in addressing the audience –, its mediality is the interplay of cinematography and theatricality, its temporality is the navigation between the epochs, its audience strategy is the mobilisation of a viewing experience between exploration, attraction and archaeology. Its texture resembles that of a *Mille-feuille* which layers the most diverse traditions of popular entertainment: from variety, the fairground, the circus and street theatre, through stage magic, the freak show and *Grand Guignol*, to those anterooms in the brothels where early pornographic scenes were projected at the beginning of the 20th century. In *Crazy Cinématographe*, performers on the wooden screen are driven to optimum performance by whippings, and in the erotic show historical Magic Lantern slides showing the sexual escapades of the Bavarian *bon viveur* Herr von Fix are presented as an intermezzo.

In comparison with historical fairground cinema, the strategies of communication are adapted for present-day audiences – for example with regard to the curatorial genre preferences. With some films, the attention mode has shifted over the historical distance: the Luxembourgian phantom ride DAS MALERIS-CHE LUXEMBURG, a local film made in 1912, is more likely to trigger contemplative absorption than kinetic immersion a century later. *Crazy Cinématographe* constructs its historical model to the same extent that it reconstructs it. In a fundamental way, however, its polymorphous economy of attention latches on to that "primitive diversity" (Alexander Kluge) which was characteristic of historical fairground cinema.[43] It has, in the light of the pixel worlds of the post-modern age, become uncharted territory again.

Translated from German by Keith Semple

Notes

1. Cf. Georg Franck, *Ökonomie der Aufmerksamkeit. Ein Entwurf* (Munich: Carl Hanser, 1998).

2. On the sociological and performative key concepts of *Crazy Cinématographe*, cf. Claude Bertemes, "Cinématographe Reloaded. Notes on the Fairground Cinema Project *Crazy Cinématographe*" in Martin Loiperdinger (ed.), *Travelling Cinema in Europe. Sources and Perspectives* (Frankfurt am Main / Basel: Stroemfeld, 2008), 190–210.

3. The term "anthropotechnique" was coined by Peter Sloterdijk – cf. Idem, *Du mußt dein Leben ändern: Über Anthropotechnik* (Frankfurt am Main: Suhrkamp, 2009).

4. In terms of the philosophy of history, the 19th century – in Benjamin's work 19th-century Paris – was explained as, so to speak, the long childhood of the 20th century.

5. Susanne Kaufmann: *Mit Walter Benjamin im Théâtre Moderne oder: Die unheimliche Moderne* (Würzburg: Königshausen & Neumann, 2002), 90–91.

6. Cf. Thomas Morsch, "Die Macht der Bilder, Spektakularisierung und die Somatisierung des Blicks im Actionkino", *Film und Kritik* 4 (October 1999), 21-43.

7. Cf. Elsaesser's reference to a "theory of spectatorship that combines the mode of distraction with that of immersion" – Thomas Elsaesser, "Archaeologies of Interactivity: Early Cinema, Narrative and Spectatorship" in Annemone Ligensa and Klaus Kreimeier (eds), *Film 1900. Technology, Perception, Culture* (New Barnet: John Libbey, 2009), 9–21 (here: 13).

8. Distraction is therefore a mode which, diagnostically as regards time, was equated directly with the onset of the modern age, for example by Georg Simmel: "The psychological foundation of the metropolitan personality type is the *increase in nervous life*, which emerges out of the rapid and unbroken change in external and internal stimuli". (Georg Simmel, "Die Großstädte und das Geistesleben" in Idem, *Soziologische Ästhetik*, Klaus Lichtblau (ed.), (Bodenheim: Wissenschaftliche Buchgesellschaft, 1998), 119–133, here: 119.)

9. For both genres, a mixed form of concentration and immersion can be assumed. In respect of *actualités*, this would be the simultaneity of informational processing on the one hand and – in the case of war scenes, for example – of immersive exposure to the explosive, spectacular happenings on the other. With regard to the local films, it would be the simultaneity of concentrated exploration and identification of familiar built-up streets, squares and buildings or trusted people from the circle of acquaintances on the one hand, and the heightening of the trusted and familiar via the screen dimension into an immersive larger-than-life experience on the other.

10. Aura, according to Benjamin's canonical definition in his *Short Story of Photography*, is the "unique apparition of a *distance*, however close it may be" [our emphasis].

11. Ben Singer, "The Ambimodernity of Early Cinema. Problems and Paradoxes in the Film-and-Modernity Discourse" in Ligensa and Kreimeier, 37–51 (here: 46). Cf. also Artaud's argument: "Il est certain que toute image, la plus sèche, la plus banale, arrive transposée sur l'écran. Le plus petit détail, l'objet le plus insignifiant prennent un sens et une vie qui leur appartiennent en propre". (Antonin Artaud, "Sorcellerie et cinéma" (1927) in Idem, *Oeuvres*, (Paris: Gallimard, 2004), 256-258, here: 257).

12. Harald Neumeyer, *Der Flaneur. Konzeptionen der Moderne* (Würzburg: Königshausen & Neumann, 1999), 29.

13. Of course it seems reasonable to assume that in sociological terms, such an attitude is more widespread in the middle classes' attention-related habitus than in that of the lower classes. One should, however, guard against generalisations of this kind, as well as the overhasty assumption that the fairground cinema audiences were mostly dominated by proletarian strata – cf. Garncarz' conclusion that the fairground cinemas' programmes were aimed at "women, men, youths and children from all social strata" (Joseph Garncarz, *Maßlose Unterhaltung. Zur Etablierung des Films in Deutschland 1896-1914*, Frankfurt am Main / Basel: Stroemfeld, 2010, 125).

14. Singer, "The Ambimodernity of Early Cinema", 43.

15. "Seemingly" because the show's dramaturgy follows an established scenario despite the improvisation.

16. Vanessa Toulmin is Research Director at the National Fairground Archive, University of Sheffield.

17. The dialectical point is that doing without a historicising perspective brings the *Crazy Cinématographe* project closer to the historical truth of fairground cinema: audiences around the turn of the 20th century, of course, experienced fairground cinema not as a historical medium but as the opposite, a new, innovative medium. With this in mind, a significant objective of the project is to communicate fairground cinema to present-day audiences, by analogy with historical ones, as an experience in which the moment of the novel, the never seen before, dominates.

18. From the turn of the century onwards, separate, fireproof projection booths came to predominate – cf. Garncarz, *Maßlose Unterhaltung*, 86.

19. Ibid., 85–86.

20. This is a reference to the concept of the *Crazy Duel*, in which local heroes take on heroes of the screen from the early cinema era: e.g. the "strongest man in the world", the Luxembourgian Guinness Book of Records record-holder Georges Christen, against 'The Acrobatic Fly', the

dumbbell-lifting star of THE ACROBATIC FLY directed by Percy Smith (GB 1908), or the duel between the Luxembourgian magician and escapologist David Goldrake and Harry Houdini.

21. Garncarz, *Maßlose Unterhaltung*, 111.

22. Cf. FÜTTERUNG VON RIESENSCHLANGEN (*Feeding Constrictors*, Germany, 1911) in the *Cabinet of Crazy Animals* programme: a scene and its exposition – white rabbits hop unsuspectingly between lurking boas – initially exudes Hitchcock-like suspense before later, when the rabbits disappear agonisingly slowly into snakes' mouths, turning into hypnotic cruelty.

23. This means that a paradigm reduced to genre analysis pure and simple can, for example, hardly explain why particular thematic programmes in *Crazy Cinématographe* – e.g. the *Comedy & Burlesque* module or the *Magical Mystery Tour* module – have been experienced as extremely rich in variety. The methodological deficiencies of the genre approach can be explained by referring to two blind spots. One is the – often attributable to an accompanying quantitative approach – suppression of the possible differentiation of a particular genre not merely into sub-genres but into a "mutant-rich", phenomenologically enigmatic spectrum of individual cases, or to put it another way: the dogmatisation of the industrial standardisation processes in early cinema and the underestimation of its archaic realm of freedom. Secondly, the differentiating and individualising scope that the film narrators have at their disposal is systematically suppressed.

24. Although confirmed by empirical findings, the method is of course subjective, up to a particular extend, if not intuitive in relation to the concrete interpretation of the audience reactions and "atmosphere" in the tent. In addition, the respective imputations are estimated average values which can vary from show to show. To sum up, the positions in the matrix are approximate.

25. In general, however, the above descriptions of the individual show elements already contain implicit references to the explanation of their attention-grabbing mode.

26. Not least because the *Crazy Pot-Pourri* spectators are traditionally a rather reserved, classical family-based audience – in contrast to the late-evening erotica module, into which a partially tipsy audience rushes in a mood of Dionysian anticipation.

27. In contrast to another, still anonymous serpentine dance film that was shown in the *Crazy Pot-Pourri* in 2007 and whose quality was that of an almost abstract movement and colour spectacle – and thereby opened the door slightly to an immersive experience.

28. Cf. Garncarz, 21.

29. This is the legendary scene involving the spacecraft stewardess, who is carrying a tray of food along a corridor wearing velcro-equipped shoes and then walks up a circular wall in an anti-clockwise direction. Cf. Brooke's description (www.screenonline.org.uk/film/id/727647/index.html). The sustained illusory power of this simple trick is documented by the contribution posted by the YouTube user redDL89, who even in 2009 was moved by this clip to ask: "How did that 'walk around the circle thing' work? Artificial gravity produced by centripetal force?"

30. The essential difference from Kubrick is that Booth did not rotate the camera in a fluid movement. Instead, in combination with a stop trick, he simply tilted it, thereby accepting a disruptive hiatus between the real world and the world of illusion. UPSIDE DOWN also comes off considerably worse when compared with films from early cinema in which gravity is suspended (e.g. Segundo de Chomon's LES KIRIKI, ACROBATS JAPONAIS, 1907 – a film from the *Crazy Pot-Pourri* module in 2007). It is, however, also considerably older.

31. Robin Curtis and Christine Voss, "Introduction", *montage AV* 17.2 (2008), 12.

32. As already expounded in the comparison between UPSIDE DOWN and L'HOMME QUI MARCHE SUR LA TÊTE.

33. Cf. Bertemes, "Cinématographe Reloaded",198.

34. Most of these films were produced between 1899 and 1906 and were shot by the cameraman Clément Maurice – cf. Tiago Baptista: "'Il faut voir le maître', A Recent Restoration of Surgical Films by E.-L. Doyen (1859–1916)", *Journal of Film Preservation* 70 (2005), 43.

35. E.g. the piece of cotton wool soaked with chloroform that is pressed regularly onto the patient's face, or the fact that Dr Doyen, at least in the early films, operates without gloves and with an imposing uncovered beard.

36. The film was probably shot by Doyen himself – cf. the accompanying copy for the film published on the *IWF Wissen und Medien* website, which Professor W. Haase wrote in 1941 for the

Reichsanstalt für Film und Bild in Wissenschaft und Unterricht, the German Reich office for film and pictures in academia and education.

37. Haase even complained that "the film isn't a real operation film as understood today, because the operation area is hardly recognisable due to its smallness" – cf. ibid.

38. E.g. the instructions "Swab please, we've run out of cooling fluid here!" or "Splendid, the cables have all been stripped! Quick, give me the saw, I'll remove his wheel axle now" delivered in a thick German accent.

39. The impression conveyed is that of a burlesque mixture of Buster Keaton's bodily eccentricity and Chaplin's criticism of industrial objectification in MODERN TIMES. It is also enriched by a hint of necrophile erotica thanks to the deathly-pale immaculacy of the motionless woman's body, which often led to the false identification of LA NOUVELLE TABLE D'OPÉRATION as belonging to the genre of early erotic film.

40. Compared with the other *Crazy Cinématographe* modules (except for the erotica module), this is the most accentuated intervention of all by the film narrators.

41. This, incidentally, is nothing more than a recourse to the historical truth: by virtue of its precisely thought-out speed and economy of gesture, Doyen's surgical technique was *de facto* patient-friendly and a breakthrough on the road to modern surgery.

42. To do this, she quotes verbatim from the meticulous descriptions of the films that Doyen wrote himself after he had handed over the distribution of his films to the *Société Générale des Cinématographes Éclipse* in 1906. By taking this step, Doyen was trying to restrict the showing of his films, which from then on he compiled in three thematic groups, to academically and scientifically oriented *conférences cinématographiques*. He did not succeed in this, however, and as early as 1907 the first compilation was sold to a French fairground showman – cf. Thierry Lefebvre, "La collection des films du Dr Doyen" in *1895*, 17 (1994), 110. Doyen's complete film descriptions, which bear the title "L'enseignement de la technique opératoire par les projections animées", are available as a download on the website of the Paris-based *Bibliothèque interuniversitaire de médecine* (www.bium.univ-paris5.fr).

43. The primitive diversity of early cinema, however, should not be confused with post-modern plasticity – with that "liquid life" which the Polish sociologist Zygmunt Bauman theorised about as the signature of the post-modern age (cf. Zygmunt Bauman, *Liquid Life*, Cambridge: Polity Press, 2005). It is rather the direct antithesis to the shapelessness of the liquid life, to its "white noise".

Dick Tomasovic

The *Crazy Cinématographe,* or the Art of the Impromptu Spectator

I t's a Sunday in early September. The sun, peeking through the clouds, has
persuaded families that it would be a fine day for a stroll on the Schueberfouer, the great outdoor fair in the city of Luxemburg. With an amused or
undecided air, you survey the stands of itinerant hawkers of cakes of soap,
liqueurs and embroidered bonnets as you walk to the rhythm, regular enough
not to annoy you, of the long, disorderly lines of people. The knife seller seems
to call out to you, but his voice is drowned out by the blaring music and the
mirthful and at the same time hysterical screams of the girls held prisoner in a
fairground attraction whose cabins and arms are whirling about a few dozen
metres over your head. The crowd becomes thicker in the narrow alleyways of
the fair and at times you have difficulty making your way without being tripped
up by the wheels of a baby carriage crossing your path. The smell of food, sweet
or savoury but most often greasy, constantly tempts or nauseates you, and you
begin to feel a little tired from the overload of sounds and sights produced by
the countless rides and attractions (the bright, stroboscopic lights of the
merry-go-round, the popular songs, the hyperbolic jingles and the slogans
shouted out by the stall keepers), of which you are the quite willing victim.
Suddenly, a young man in the crowd grabs your attention and hands you a little
piece of paper, on which is written the big word Cinematograph, and you
follow him to a tent a few metres farther on that you hadn't noticed before.
The young man abandons you, but facing you on a narrow platform, battling
the decibels flying from the shooting range located across the way, two barkers,
gleefully bickering, describe in Homeric terms the films being shown inside
the tent. They urge you on: the show is about to start and – what, you haven't
got your ticket? – you rush to the ticket counter, take a few more steps, proffer
your ticket in exchange for a fan and penetrate the semi-darkness of the warm
lair of the *Crazy Cinématographe*. To your right, a raised projector appears ready

---

Facing page:
Upper: Front-show announcing a *Crazy Erotique* late night performance.
Lower: To Demonstrate How Spiders Fly (Great Britain 1909), performed within the *Cabinet of
Crazy Animals* programme, *Schueberfouer* 2008.

to roar. In front of you the screen, and a little in-between space where the two barkers are noisily at work, inviting the spectators to take a seat on one of the wooden benches. "Come in, come in", and in you come. "Squeeze in a little more, squeeze in a little more", and you squeeze in a little more in the midst of these strangers who, like you, already seem to be enchanted by the mere incongruity of being in such a place. You're thinking of Victor Hugo, of his idea of feeling alone together, of the fact that he died just before the invention of the cinematograph, when you become aware of the pianist nestled behind his keyboard and his joyful improvisation at the piano next to the screen. "Attention! attention!", and you pay attention. "Are you ready?" Yes, you're ready, and like the others you answer that you're ready, without quite knowing whether you are or what you're ready for. The projector starts up, the screen lights up and the lecturers welcome the first images of a hundred-year-old black-and-white film with delirious enthusiasm and for a brief, tender moment, but without any doubt, you sense that your neighbours, young and old, breathe a sigh of joy and amazement, almost as if they were discovering moving images for the first time, which is clearly not at all the case. You then think of Jules Romains' poems on fairground attractions and, particularly, his poem about the crowds at the cinematograph:

> A bright circle abruptly illuminates the far wall. The whole room seems to sigh, 'Ah!' And through the surprise simulated by this cry, they welcome the resurrection they were certain would come. The group dream now begins.[1]

Twenty minutes later, after quite a bit of musical whimsy from the pianist, wisecracks from the lecturers and gags on screen from the slapstick films, and after having applauded, thanked and paid your respects, you leave through an exit located behind the projector. Gradually, you return to daylight, to the cool air and the deafening noise of the fairground, which you had succeeded in putting on hold during the film screening. You rejoin the flowing crowd. You're back in the city.

★ ★ ★

While the *Crazy Cinématographe* project is remarkable in many respects (for its archaeological concerns alongside its contemporary re-reading of the early film show; the quality of its lecturers and screening conditions; the talent of its pianists; the motivation of the people behind it; the charm of the big tent; and, of course, the variety of its film programs) its principal quality is undoubtedly the unique, complex, entertaining and inquiring spectatorial experience it offers. Indeed *Crazy Cinématographe* spectators are at one and the same time gawkers, idlers, onlookers, courtroom spectators, discoverers and witnesses: hypothetical spectators who are neither the focused and silent spectator of the movie theatre nor the simple spectator of early fairground shows, nor the curious spectator of the film lecture, nor the spectator used to domestic screens. In truth, these spectators' singularity lies in traversing, during the *Crazy Cinématographe* show, the range of manifestations and temporalities of their condition as *impromptu* spectators.

Because of the diversity of personalities involved and their experiences, and because of the irreducibility of subjectivities, describing the spectatorial condition with any precision is an impossible task. At the same time, it is worthwhile to attempt to explain the different kinds of spectatorial position brought into play to varying degrees by an experience such as that described here, in that such an attempt would use the early film strip to explore the indispensability of a history of visual culture. These spectatorial positions are numerous, overlapping and interconnected. Here I will mention three major such positions, which are complementary and inextricably linked.

First of all, the obvious status of *Crazy Cinématographe* spectators should be remarked upon: these are not cinema spectators. Or rather, they are partial, modified or metamorphosed cinema spectators. The reasons for this are many and quite apparent: they did not choose the film they are going to see, they may even not have chosen the screening time (the attraction rose up in their path); they found none of the comfort of the movie theatre or their usual bearings (a wooden bench versus a plush seat, the aggressive presence of the projector versus the soundproof projection booth, live sound versus post-synchronised soundtrack, etc.); they are often directly addressed by the film show (beginning with the harangue of the lecturer), a little like a cabaret spectator, whereas they are accustomed to forgetting about the mechanics of the screening; and, finally, the films are quite different, both in their language and in their poetics, from the films these spectators normally see in a movie theatre.

Thus depending on their knowledge of film history and the extent to which they are avid film goers, these impromptu spectators will experience varying degrees of surprise at this fairground attraction. In any event, they are quickly required to adapt to screening circumstances that are new to them, even if they are aware that they are the origin of the film screenings they attend more or less regularly. For many of these spectators, the *Crazy Cinématographe* thus offers a new and profoundly exhibitionist kind of entertainment, one that belongs to film's earliest modern paradigms of attraction and monstration. Since the work of Tom Gunning and André Gaudreault,[2] all this has become well known to film theorists and historians, but it never fails to surprise the general public. Not that these qualities (direct address, moving pictures that challenge the viewer, the autonomy of the film's *tableaux*, etc.) are unfamiliar to them (quite the contrary: the 'new media' – television, video, the Internet – indulge in them freely and contemporary cinema by no means abstains from them), but simply because they have not experienced them in this form and in this particular delivery system.[3] It is precisely in its mode of address that the *Crazy Cinématographe* throws the spectator's position into upheaval, both through the films on its programme (the specific grammar of film-as-attraction in the early cinema period) and the projection circumstances (touts, lecturers, pianist, the projectionist's presence in the room, etc.).

This upheaval is particularly apparent in the behaviour of *Crazy Cinématographe* spectators, who have just twenty minutes or so to grasp the cinematograph's

SAÏDA A ENLEVÉ MANNEKEN-PIS (France, 1913).

principles: when the screening begins they are silent, immobile and passive, according to their custom, when what is required of them is to be active and noisy and possibly to move about and be disorderly. Can they answer the lecturers' questions, injunctions and jokes? Can they remain standing? Can they leave the room during the screening? Can they comment on the screening to their neighbour? Can they or should they applaud between films, and if so, should they applaud the lecturer and pianist or the film? The interdisciplinary encounter between recorded show and live show does not occur without giving rise to a number of questions about the spectators' behaviour. They have to agree to modify their reception paradigms around the film show and their psychic predisposition to let themselves be absorbed by it.

The novelty effect of the *Crazy Cinématographe*, moreover, creates a perceptual anachronism, one that pushes the spectator, curiously enough, to become interested in questions of technology and equipment, perhaps even more so than in the content of the screening. Naturally, people will forcefully remember the films' dancing pig, the rubber man's contortionist routine, Auguste the monkey sitting down to a fine dinner, the Kiriki family's human pyramid and the way Alfred Machin's leopard raced through the streets of Brussels, but they will remember even more the shape of the tent, the size of the screen, the way the lecturer struck the screen with his cane and the sound of the projector: in short, a whole series of elements relating more to the film show than to the films' content. The projectionists have described, moreover, the interest that spectators showed in the tool of their trade, normally so well hidden and

LE ROI DES DOLLARS (France, 1905).

forgotten. We might recall that Tom Gunning has demonstrated that an emerging medium goes through a period of opacity during which its materiality is visible to such an extent that it can literally screen out its content.[4] As Isabelle Raynauld explains,[5] as viewers' skill levels increase, the opacity of the medium recedes and is replaced by transparency, making the content more visible. Curiously, *Crazy Cinématographe* spectators appear to recreate this experience dating from the emergence of early cinema. This does not mean, of course, that they are transformed into early spectators (there is no question here of recovering a kind of virginity or of reliving cinema's infancy, to use a worn-out cliché), but rather that they navigate between different moments of cultural history, superimposing the gaze of those who discovered cinema for the first time on their usual gaze. In short, the *Crazy Cinématographe* does not just show spectacular images; it creates the spectacular. It succeeds quite effectively in coming to life as an attraction.

If this film show functions, despite the way in which the spectator's normal ways of seeing are upturned, it is precisely because a second way of seeing takes their place, driven by a desire for distraction, surprise, astonishment, amazement and sensory overload; in other words, for attraction. This way of seeing is, of course, that of the fairground gawker. While we are all familiar with the importance of the concept of the *flâneur* to an understanding of urban modernity and its prominent place in the work of writers from Charles Baudelaire to

Walter Benjamin to Susan Sontag, to better understand the originality of the gaze engendered by attraction it may be worthwhile to recall the distinction made by the literary critic Victor Fournel in 1855 between the *flâneur* and the gawker (*badaud*):

> The simple *flâneur* observes and reflects; or at least he can. He is always in full possession of his individuality. The individuality of the gawker, on the other hand, disappears and is absorbed by the outside world, which delights him to the point of delirium and ecstasy. Under the influence of spectacle, the gawker becomes an impersonal being; no longer a man, he is the public, the crowd. Nature apart, the true gawker, a keen and naïve soul taken to daydreaming, passion and agreeable enthusiasm, an artist by instinct and temperament with little experience of life, in other words having none of the scornful scepticism and unhealthy pride which, according to the moralists, are the two great scourges of our time, is worthy of the admiration of everyone whose heart is true and sincere.[6]

Ultimately, the gawkers on the *Schueberfouer* in 2010 were not so far removed from the mid-nineteenth-century Parisian described by Fournel. By the end of a process of de-individualisation, they were able to indulge in delight and suspend their scepticism, the corollary of their daily lives, habits and experiences, rediscovering a kind of guilelessness proper to amazement. Nevertheless, the *flâneur* in them, the participating and reflective observer, was never completely absent.

Indeed *Crazy Cinématographe* spectators were also ineluctably spectator-visitors. For the tent was something one visited (entering by a door, exiting by another, watching the show and its actors as if it were an installation), and few visitors would not have known that it had been organised by the Cinémathèque of the city of Luxemburg. The educational aims of the people behind it, the film descriptions posted in the entrance hall and the quite clearly reconstructed nature of the screening (the lecturers were contemporary, making jokes about the present-day Belgian political crisis, for example, during Alfred Machin's film SAÏDA A ENLEVÉ MANNEKEN-PIS, but their costumes were old-fashioned and their attitudes that of another age) situate the *Crazy Cinématographe* as a museum endeavour. Dominique Païni, writing about the mobile and solitary position of the spectator of installations and films in a museum or art gallery, employs the term *flâneur*.[7] In the present case the *flâneur*, made momentarily captive by the film show, joins the cinema spectator. The performance, comic and museum aspects of *Crazy Cinématographe* blend into one another, inviting the spectator to adopt various ways of looking.

One might add a few additional kinds of spectatorial position of varying importance to the three described here: the courtroom spectator or witness who attends a fleeting process of recreating a historical entertainment practice; the actively present spectator of performance and live entertainment; and the all-encompassing and distanced position of the practised viewer of domestic screens (given the narrow dimensions of the *Crazy Cinématographe*, its screen may not have been much bigger than the viewer's home theatre system). Of course, every spectator draws on their own ways of looking, determined by their own experiences, and it would be futile to try to list them exhaustively here. Nevertheless, as we have seen, the quite unique experience of the *Crazy Cinématographe* brings spectators into play in a quite peculiar manner, one involving both their archaeology and their reinvention.

Translated from French by Timothy Barnard

Notes

1. Jules Romains, "The Crowd at the Cinematograph" (1911), trans. Richard Abel, in Abel (ed.), *French Film Theory and Criticism, A History/Anthology*, vol. 1, 1907–1929 (Princeton: Princeton University Press, 1988), 53.

2. Cf. Tom Gunning, "The Cinema of Attraction(s): Early Film, Its Spectator and the Avant-Garde" in Thomas Elsaesser (ed.), *Early Cinema: Space, Frame, Narrative* (London: BFI, 1990); and André Gaudreault and Tom Gunning, "Early Cinema as a Challenge to Film History", trans. Joyce Goggin and Wanda Strauven, in Strauven (ed.), *The Cinema of Attractions Reloaded* (Amsterdam: Amsterdam University Press, 2006), 365–380.

3. For a number of discussions of the cinema of attractions concept, see Wanda Strauven (ed.), *The Cinema of Attractions Reloaded* (Amsterdam: Amsterdam University Press, 2006).

4. Tom Gunning, "Re-Newing Old Technologies: Astonishment, Second Nature, and the Uncanny in Technology from the Previous Turn-of-the-Century", in David Thorburn and Henry Jenkins (eds), *Rethinking Media Change: The Aesthetics of Transition* (Cambridge: MIT Press, 2003), 39–60.

5. Isabelle Raynauld, "Le cinématographe comme nouvelle technologie: opacité et transparence", *CiNéMAS* 14.1 (2003): 117–128.

6. Victor Fournel, *Ce qu'on voit dans les rues de Paris* (Paris: Dentu Libraire-éditeur, 1867 [1855]), 270.

7. Dominique Païni, *Le temps exposé: Le cinéma de la salle au musée* (Paris: Cahiers du Cinéma, 2002), 54.

Upper: ANARKISTENS SVIGERMODER
Lower: BONSOIR [TABLEAU FLEURI]

Claude Bertemes, Nicole Dahlen

The Art of Crazy Programming
Documentation of *Crazy Cinématographe*
Programmes, 2007 to 2010

**Crazy Cinématographe Programme Modules as Performed on the
Luxembourg Fairground *Schueberfouer* 2007–2010**

Schueberfouer 2007

Dates: 23 August to 11 September
Number of showings: 152
Total entries: 9,374

Crazy Pot-Pourri

Concours de gourmands, France 1905, Comedy
Agoust Family of Jugglers, Great Britain 1898, Vaudeville Act
The Adventures of 'Wee Rob Roy' No.1, Great Britain 1916, Animated Film
[Dansa Serpentina], France 1900, Dance Film
Le Cochon danseur, France 1907, Vaudeville Act
Dévaliseurs nocturnes, France 1904, Comedy
Les Kiriki, acrobates japonais, France 1907, Trick Film
Großer Blumen-Corso 1906, Luxembourg 1906, Topical / local film

Cabinet of the Bizarre

Photographie d'une étoile, France 1906, Comedy
L'Homme mystérieux, France 1910, Vaudeville Act
Fox terriers et rats, France c1902, Topical
Dr Macintyre's X-Ray Film, Great Britain 1896/c1909, Scientific Film
Dr Macintyre's X-Ray Cabinet, Great Britain c1909, Scientific Film
[Hunde-Theater], France c1907, Vaudeville Animal Act
Kobelkoff, France 1900, Vaudeville Act
Miss Harry's femme serpent, France 1911, Vaudeville Act

Comedy & Burlesque

Anarkistens Svigermoder, Denmark 1906, Comedy
Une idylle sous un tunnel, France 1901, Comedy
Arthème avale sa clarinette, France 1912, Comedy

La Course à la perruque, France 1906, Chase Film
Acrobati comici, Italy 1910, Vaudeville Act
Horrible fin d'un concierge, France 1903, Comedy
Lèvres collées, France 1906, Comedy
Fâcheuse méprise, France 1905, Comedy

Magical Mystery Tour

Le Roi des Dollars, France 1905, Trick Film
Les Tulipes, France 1907, *Féerie*
Le Barbier fin de siècle, France 1896, Trick Film
La Poule phénomène, France 1905, Trick Film
Voyage autour d'une étoile, France 1906, *Féerie*
The ? Motorist, Great Britain 1906, Trick Film

The Sex Lives of our Grandparents

Le Réveil de Chrysis, France c1897/99, Erotic Scene
Das eitle Stubenmädchen, Austria 1908/10, Erotic Scene
Bains des dames de la cour, France 1904, Erotic Scene
[Scène Pornographique], France 1909, Semi-pornographic Film
Weibliche Assertierung, Austria 1908/1910, Erotic Scene
Mousquetaire au restaurant, France 1920, Pornographic Film
Au revoir et merci, France 1906, Comedy

Schueberfouer 2008

> Dates: 22 August to 10 September
> Number of showings: 153
> Total entries: 7,531

Crazy Pot-Pourri

Danse serpentine, France c1897, Danse Film
Chiens savants: la danse serpentine, France 1898, Vaudeville Animal Act
Upside Down: or, The Human Flies, Great Britain 1899, Trick Film
L'Homme qui marche sur la tête, France 1909, Vaudeville Act
La Peine du talion, France 1906, *Féerie*
Théâtre de Hula-Hula, c1917, Animated Film
Jubileusz 3-lecia klubu sportowego "Victoria" w Czêstochowie [fragment: Athlete Rupprecht], Poland c1910, Topical
Première sortie d'une cycliste, France 1907, Comedy
Les Six Soeurs Dainef, France 1902, Vaudeville Act
Sur les remparts de Luxembourg, France c1919, Travelogue
Bonsoir [tableau fleuri], France 1906, Trick Film

Cabinet of Crazy Animals

Chiens savants: équilibres, France 1899, Vaudeville Animal Act
Les Chats boxeurs, France 1898, Vaudeville Animal Act
Das boxende Känguruh, Germany 1895, Vaudeville Animal Act

Upper: EFFETI DI UN RAZZO
Lower: EN AVANT LA MUSIQUE

Madame Babylas aime les animaux, France 1911, Comedy
[Unter dem Mikroskop. Larve der Wasserfliege], Great Britain 1903, Scientific Film
Fütterung von Riesenschlangen, Germany 1911, Topical
Hurdle Jumping by Trained Dogs, USA 1899, Vaudeville Animal Act
Bicyclette présentée en liberté, France 1906, Vaudeville Act
"King" and "Queen", the Great High Diving Horses, USA 1899, Topical
To Demonstrate How Spiders Fly, Great Britain 1909, Animated Film
The Acrobatic Fly, Great Britain 1910, Scientific Film

Comedy & Burlesque

La Crinoline, France 1906, Comedy
Chirurgie fin de siècle, France 1900, Trick Film
[Upside-Down Boxers], Great Britain 1899, Vaudeville Act
La Course aux potirons, France 1907, Chase Film
Erreur de porte, France 1904, Comedy
Bain de pieds à la moutarde, France c1902, Comedy
Les Maçons, France 1905, Comedy
Chez le dentiste, France 1907, Comedy
Bonsoir [loge de théâtre], France 1906

The Sex Lives of our Grandparents

[La Coiffure], France c1905, Erotic Scene
[Erotische Filmfragmenten: Topless exotiques], Country/Year: Unknown, Erotic Scene
La Confession, France 1905, Comedy
Baden verboten, Austria 1906/08, Erotic Scene
Le Satyre Casimir, France c1930, Pornographic Film
Buried Treasure, USA 1925, Pornographic Animated Film
Le Thermomètre de l'amour, France 1906, Comedy

Schueberfouer 2009

    Dates: 21 August to 9 September
    Number of showings: 152
    Total entries: 8,932

Crazy Pot-Pourri

Arroseur et arrosé, III, France c1897, Comedy [2 days only]
The Twins' Tea Party, Great Britain 1896, Facial Expression Film
L'Equilibre impossible, France 1902, Trick Film
Double saut périlleux (II), France 1899, Vaudeville Act
En avant la musique, France 1907, Trick Film
Excelsior!, France 1901, Trick Film
Leap Frog, Great Britain 1900, Topical
That Fatal Sneeze, Great Britain 1907, Chase Film/Trick Film
Un homme de tête, France 1898, Trick Film

Sauts périlleux par deux (III), France 1899, Vaudeville Act
Bonsoir [la fée aux fleurs], France 1906, Trick Film

Cabinet of the Bizarre & Extraordinary

The Big Swallow, Great Britain 1901, Trick Film
The Strength and Agility of Insects, Great Britain 1911, Scientific Film
Spiders on a Web, Great Britain 1900, Scientific Film
Dislocation mystérieuse, France 1906, Trick Film
Die Schlangentänzerin, Germany 1909, Vaudeville Act
Tom Pouce suit une femme, France 1910, Comedy
Le Déjeuner du savant, France 1905, Comedy [2 days only]
Comment on attrape les maladies contagieuses. Comment on les évite, France 1919, Educational Film
Sauts périlleux (I), France 1899, Vaudeville Act
Ecriture à l'envers, France 1896, Vaudeville Act

Comedy & Burlesque

Explosion of a Motor Car, Great Britain 1900, Trick Film
Les Anglais en voyage: II. Pirouettes et sauts périlleux, France 1897, Vaudeville Act
Premier prix de violoncelle, France 1907, Comedy
Les Effets du melon, France 1906, Comedy
Effeti di un razzo, Italy 1911, Comedy
Nouvelles luttes extravagantes, France 1901, Trick Film
Mary Jane's Mishap or, Don't Fool with the Paraffin, Great Britain 1903, Trick Film [2 days only]
Les Anglais en voyage: III. Pirouettes et sauts périlleux, France 1897, Vaudeville Act
Le Réveil d'un monsieur pressé, France 1900, Trick Film

Le Cabinet chirurgical du Dr Doyen

Chirurgie fin de siècle, France 1900, Trick Film
Unterschenkelamputation, Germany c1903, Scientific Film
[Der neue Behandlungsstuhl], France c1915, Scientific Film
Extirpation d'un kyste du corps thyroïde, France 1898/1903, Scientific Film
Extirpation d'une tumeur du testicule, France 1898/1903, Scientific Film
Chirurgie mécanique, I, France c1903, Comedy

Erotique 1900

La Belle di Miranda in ihrer Scene: Nach der Reitübung, Germany 1906, Erotic Scene
[Besuch im Badezimmer], France c1904, Comedy
Akt-Skulpturen. Studienfilm für bildende Künstler, Germany 1903, Erotic Scene
[Scène Pornographique], France 1909, Semi-pornographic Film
L'Abbé Bitt au couvent, France 1925, Pornographic Film
[Erotische Filmfragmenten: Adoration érotique], Country/Year: Unknown, Erotic Scene

Let me dream again, Great Britain 1900, Comedy
On doit le dire, France 1918, Educational Film [1 day only]

Schueberfouer 2010

> Dates: 20 August to 8 September
> Number of showings: 155
> Total entries: 7,585

Cabinet Fantastico

La Poule phénomène, France 1905, Trick Film
Le Singe "August", France 1904, Vaudeville Animal Act
Les Œufs de Pâques, France 1907, Trick Film
L'Homme mystérieux, France 1910, Vaudeville Act
L'Illusionniste double et la tête vivante, France 1900, Trick Film
Le Cochon danseur, France 1907, Vaudeville Act

Comedy & Burlesque

Concours de gourmands, France 1905, Comedy
Les Mésaventures d'un cycliste myope, France 1907, Comedy
Les Kiriki, acrobates japonais, France 1907, Trick Film
[Pumpstation für Radfahrer], France 1906, Comedy
Saïda a enlevé Manneken-Pis, France 1913, Comedy

Erotique 1900

Après le bal, France 1897, Erotic Scene
Der Hausarzt, Austria 1908-1910, Erotic Scene
Fix's Hôtel-Abenteuer, Germany c1890, Series of 10 Pornographic
  Magic Lantern Slides
Les Filles de Loth, France c1925, Pornographic Film
L'Eclipse du soleil en pleine lune [fragment], France 1907, Trick Film

★ ★ ★

Crazy Cinématographe is a fairground cinema project of the Cinémathèque de la Ville de Luxembourg, realized with the help of the following film archives:

> Association Frères Lumière, BFI National Archive, Bundesarchiv-Filmarchiv, CNA Luxembourg, Cinemateca Portuguesa, Cinematek – Cinémathèque royale de Belgique, Cinémathèque française, CNC – Archives françaises du film, Danish Film Institute, Deutsche Kinemathek – Museum für Film und Fernsehen, Deutsches Filminstitut – DIF, EYE Film Institute Netherlands, Filmarchiv Austria, Filmoteca de Catalunya, Filmoteca de Zaragoza, Filmoteca Española, Filmoteka Narodowa, Gaumont Pathé Archives, George Eastman House, La Cinémathèque de Toulouse, Lobster Films, Österreichisches Filmmuseum, Scottish Film Archive.

Upper: FÂCHEUSE MÉPRISE
Lower: MADAME BABYLAS AIME LES ANIMAUX

DVD *Crazy Cinématographe. Europäisches Jahrmarktkino 1896-1916* (Edition Filmmuseum #18)

DVD 1: European Cinema of Attractions, 1896–1916

Will Evans, the Musical Eccentric, Great Britain 1899, Vaudeville Act
Anarkistens Svigermoder, Denmark 1906, Comedy
[Dansa Serpentina], France 1900, Dance Film
Le Roi des Dollars, France 1905, Trick Film
L'Homme mystérieux, France 1910, Vaudeville Act
Le Réveil de Chrysis, France c1897/99, Erotic Scene
Premier prix de violoncelle, France 1907, Comedy
Agoust Family of Jugglers, Great Britain 1898, Vaudeville Act
Les Tulipes, France 1907, *Féerie*
Dr Macintyre's X-Ray Film, Great Britain 1896/c1909, Scientific Film
Dr Macintyre's X-Ray Cabinet, Great Britain c1909, Scientific Film
Bains des dames de la cour, France 1904, Erotic Scene
The Adventures of "Wee Rob Roy" No.1, Great Britain 1916, Animated Film
Les Kiriki, acrobates japonais, France 1907, Trick Film
The ? Motorist, Great Britain 1906, Trick Film
Photographie d'une étoile, France 1906, Comedy
[Hunde-Theater], France c1907, Vaudeville Animal Act
Horrible fin d'un concierge, France 1903, Comedy
A Peace of Coal, Great Britain c1910, Animated Film
Miss Harry's femme serpent, France 1911, Vaudeville Act
Bain de pieds à la moutarde, France c1902, Comedy
[Scène Pornographique], France 1909, Semi-pornographic Film
L'Amblystôme, France 1913, Scientific Film
Le Barbier fin de siècle, France 1896, Trick Film
Lèvres collées, France 1906, Comedy
The Tale of the Ark, Great Britain 1909, Animated Film
Fâcheuse méprise, France 1905, Comedy
Sculpteur moderne, France 1908, Trick Film
Acrobati comici, Italy 1910, Vaudeville Act
Fox terriers et rats, France c1902, Topical
Saïda a enlevé Manneken-Pis, France 1913, Comedy
Au revoir et merci, France 1906, Comedy

DVD 2: Local Films from the Greater Region, 1902–1914

Das malerische Luxemburg / Le Luxembourg pittoresque, Luxembourg 1912, Phantom ride / local film
St. Willibrordus-Feierlichkeiten zu Echternach 1906 aka *Übertragung der Reliquien des hl. Willibrod in die Basilika*, Luxembourg 1906, Topical / local film
Große Springprozession 1906 / La Procession Dansante d'Echternach 1906, Luxem-

bourg 1906, Topical

Oktav-Prozession 1911 / Procession de l'Octave 1911, Luxembourg 1911, Topical / local film

Große Cavalcade zu Luxembourg 1905 / Cavalcade à Luxembourg 1905, Luxembourg 1905, Topical / local film

Großer Blumen-Corso 1906 / Fête des Fleurs 1906, Luxembourg 1906, Topical / local film

Die Beisetzungsfeierlichkeiten S.K.H. des Großherzogs Wilhelm IV / Les funérailles de S.A.R. le Grand-Duc de Luxembourg, Luxembourg 1912, Topical / local film

Die Thronbesteigung der Kronprinzessin Maria-Adelheid von Luxemburg / Fêtes de l'avènement de S.A.R. la Grand-Duchesse Marie-Adelaïde de Luxembourg, Luxembourg 1912, Topical / local film

[S.A.R. Marie-Adélaïde au cinéma], Luxembourg 1912, Topical / local film

Ein Besuch in der Champagnerfabrik E. Mercier u. Cie zu Luxemburg, sowie in deren großartigen Etablissements und Weiden-Anlagen in Kopstal / La fabrication Champagne Mercier, Luxembourg 1907, Industrial Film / local film

[Autofahrt durch Trier], Germany c1903, Phantom ride / local film

[Domausgang in Trier 1904], Germany 1904, Topical / local film

Domausgang am Ostersonntag, Germany 1909, Topical / local film

Fronleichnamsprozession in Trier, Germany 1909, Topical / local film

[Bilder aus Trier], Germany 1902-1909, Travelogue / local film

Leben und Treiben auf dem Viehmarkt am 5. Mai. Bekannte Trierer Handels-Typen im Wirken, Germany 1909, Topical / local film

Blumenkorso 1914, veranstaltet vom Radfahrerverein Trier, gegr. 1885, Germany 1914, Topical / local film

[Street Scenes in Saarbrücken], Germany 1909, Phantom ride / local film

Filmography Crazy Cinématographe 2007–2010

L'Abbé Bitt au couvent, France 1925, Length: 99 m, b&w, Origin: Lobster Films

Acrobati comici, Italy 1910, Prod: Cines, Length: 95 m, b&w, Origin: Cinematek – Cinémathèque royale de Belgique

The Acrobatic Fly, Great Britain 1910, Prod: Charles Urban Trading Co, Dir: Percy Smith, Length: 53 m, b&w, Origin: BFI National Archive

The Adventures of 'Wee Rob Roy' No.1, Great Britain 1916, Length: 64 m, b&w, Origin: Scottish Screen Archive

Agoust Family of Jugglers, Great Britain 1898, Prod: British Mutoscope and Biograph Company, Dir: Anonymous, Length: 12 m, b&w, Origin: EYE Film Institute Netherlands

Akt-Skulpturen. Studienfilm für bildende Künstler, Germany 1903, Prod: Messter's Projektion GmbH, Length: 31 m, b&w, Origin: Deutsche Kinemathek

L'Amblystôme, France 1913, Prod: Eclair / Scientia, Length: 120 m, b&w, Origin: CNC – Archives françaises du film

Anarkistens Svigermoder, Denmark 1906, Prod: Nordisk Films Kompagni, Dir: Viggo Larsen, b&w, Length: 71 m, Origin: Danish Film Institute

Les Anglais en voyage: II. Pirouettes et sauts périlleux, France 1897, Prod: Lumière, Length: 16 m, b&w, Origin: CNC – Archives françaises du film

Les Anglais en voyage: III. Pirouettes et sauts périlleux, France 1897, Prod: Lumière, Length: 17 m, b&w, Origin: CNC – Archives françaises du film

Après le bal, France 1897, Prod: Star-Film, Dir: Georges Méliès, Length: 20 m, b&w, Origin: Lobster Films

Arroseur et arrosé, III, France c1897, Prod: Lumière, Length: 14 m, b&w, Origin: CNC – Archives françaises du film

Arthème avale sa clarinette, France 1912, Prod: Société Générale des Cinématographes Éclipse, Dir: Ernest Servaès, Length: 80 m, b&w, Origin: Lobster Films

Athlete Rupprecht cf. Jubileusz 3-lecia klubu sportowego "Victoria" w Częstochowie.

Au revoir et merci, France 1906, Prod: Pathé, Dir: Anonymous, Length: 37 m, b&w, Origin: Filmarchiv Austria

[Autofahrt durch Trier], Germany c1903, Prod: Marzen, Edison's Elektrisches Theater, Length: 29 m, b&w, Origin: Bundesarchiv-Filmarchiv

Baden verboten, Austria 1906/08, Prod: Saturn-Film, Dir: Johann Schwarzer, Length: 20 m, b&w, Origin: Filmarchiv Austria

Bain de pieds à la moutarde, France c1902, Prod: Parnaland, Length: 34 m, b&w, Origin: Filmoteca de Catalunya

Bains des dames de la cour, France 1904, Prod: Pathé, Dir: Anonymous, Length: 19 m, b&w, Origin: Filmoteca de Zaragoza / Filmoteca Española

Upper: ŒUFS DE PACQUES
Lower: PREMIER PRIX DE VIOLONCELLE

Le Barbier fin de siècle, France 1896, Prod: Pathé, Dir: Anonymous, Length: 14 m, b&w, Origin: Lobster Films

Die Beisetzungsfeierlichkeiten S.K.H. des Großherzogs Wilhelm IV / Les funérailles de S.A.R. le Grand-Duc de Luxembourg, Luxembourg 1912, Prod: Hubert Marzen, Parisiana, Luxembourg, Length: 82 m, b&w, Origin: CNA Luxembourg

La Belle di Miranda in ihrer Scene: Nach der Reitübung, Germany 1906, Prod: Messter's Projektion GmbH, Length: 38 m, b&w, Origin: Deutsche Kinemathek

[Besuch im Badezimmer], France c1904, Prod: Pathé, Dir: Anonymous, Length: 15 m, b&w, Origin: Deutsche Kinemathek

Ein Besuch in der Champagnerfabrik E. Mercier u. Cie zu Luxemburg, sowie in deren großartigen Etablissements und Weiden-Anlagen in Kopstal / La fabrication Champagne Mercier, Luxembourg 1907, Prod: Marzen, Edison's Elektrisches Theater, Length: 161 m, b&w, Origin: CNA Luxembourg

Bicyclette présentée en liberté, France 1906, Prod: Pathé, Dir: Gaston Velle, Length: 50 m, b&w, Origin: BFI National Archive

The Big Swallow, Great Britain 1901, Prod: Williamson Kinematograph Company, Dir: James Williamson, Length: 23 m, b&w, Origin: BFI National Archive

[Bilder aus Trier], Germany 1902-1909, Prod: Marzen, Edison's Elektrisches Theater, Length: 87 m, b&w, Origin: Bundesarchiv-Filmarchiv

Blumenkorso 1914, veranstaltet vom Radfahrerverein Trier, gegr. 1885, Germany 1914, Prod: Peter Marzen, Germania Lichtspiele, Trier, Length: 74 m, Origin: Bundesarchiv-Filmarchiv

Bonsoir [la fée aux fleurs], France 1906, Prod: Gaumont, Dir: Alice Guy, Length: 10 m, stencil-coloured, Origin: Cinematek – Cinémathèque royale de Belgique

Bonsoir [loge de théâtre], France 1906, Prod: Gaumont, Dir: Anonymous, Length: 4 m, tinted, Origin: Cinematek – Cinémathèque royale de Belgique

Bonsoir [tableau fleuri], France 1906, Prod: Gaumont, Dir: Anonymous, Length: 10 m, stencil-coloured, Origin: Cinematek – Cinémathèque royale de Belgique

Das boxende Känguruh, Germany 1895, Prod: Skladanowsky (Berlin), Dir: Max Skladanowsky, Length: 5 m, b&w, Origin: Bundesarchiv-Filmarchiv

Buried Treasure, USA 1925, Prod: Climax Fables, Length: 135 m, b&w, Origin: Lobster Films

Les Chats boxeurs, France 1898, Prod: Lumière, Length: 15 m, b&w, Origin: CNC – Archives françaises du film

Chez le dentiste, France 1907, Prod: Pathé, Dir: Anonymous, Length: 88 m, b&w, Origin: Cinematek – Cinémathèque Royale de Belgique

Chiens savants: équilibres, France 1899, Prod: Lumière, Length: 16 m, b&w, Origin: CNC – Archives françaises du film

Chiens savants: la danse serpentine, France 1898, Prod: Lumière, Length: 15 m, b&w, Origin: CNC – Archives françaises du film

Chirurgie fin de siècle, France 1900, Prod: Gaumont, Dir: Alice Guy, Length: 41 m, b&w, Origin: Lobster Films

Chirurgie mécanique, France c1903, Prod: Lumière, Length: 43 m, b&w, Origin: CNC – Archives françaises du film

Le Cochon danseur, France 1907, Prod: Pathé / S.C.A.G.L., Dir: Anonymous, Length: 81 m, b&w, Origin: Lobster Films

[La Coiffure], France c1905, Prod: Unknown, Length: 20 m, b&w, Origin: CNC – Archives françaises du film

Comment on attrape les maladies contagieuses. Comment on les évite, France 1919, Prod: Pathé, Dir: Jean Comandon, Marius O'Galop, Length: 54 m, b&w, Origin: CNC – Archives françaises du film

Concours de gourmands, France 1905, Prod: Pathé, Dir: Anonymous, Length: 28 m, b&w, Origin: Cinematek – Cinémathèque royale de Belgique

La Confession, France 1905, Prod: Pathé, Dir: Anonymous, Length: 23 m, b&w, Origin: CNC – Archives françaises du film

La Course à la perruque, France 1906, Prod: Pathé, Dir: Georges Hatot, Length: 117 m, b&w, Origin: Filmarchiv Austria

La Course aux potirons, France 1907, Prod: Gaumont, Dir: Louis Feuillade, Length: 127 m, b&w, Origin: Cinematek – Cinémathèque royale de Belgique

La Crinoline, France 1906, Prod: Gaumont, Dir: Alice Guy, Length: 35 m, b&w, Origin: Filmarchiv Austria

[Dansa Serpentina], France 1900, Prod: Gaumont, Dir: Anonymous, Length: 19 m, hand-coloured, Origin: Filmoteca de Catalunya

Danse serpentine [II], France c1897, Prod: Lumière, Length: 15 m, hand-coloured, Origin: CNC – Archives françaises du film

Le Déjeuner du savant, France 1905, Prod: Pathé, Dir: Anonymous, Length: 38 m, b&w, Origin: BFI National Archive (Joseph Joye Collection)

Dévaliseurs nocturnes, France 1904, Prod: Pathé, Dir: Gaston Velle, Length: 67 m, b&w, Origin: Filmoteca de Catalunya

Dislocation mystérieuse, France 1906, Prod: Star-Film, Dir: Georges Méliès, Length: 32 m, b&w, Origin: Lobster Films

Domausgang am Ostersonntag, Germany 1909, Prod: Marzen, Edison's Elektrisches Theater im Lokale des Central-Theaters, Trier, Length: 56 m, b&w, Origin: Bundesarchiv-Filmarchiv

[Domausgang in Trier 1904], Germany 1904, Prod: Marzen, Edison's Elektrisches Theater, Length: 29 m, b&w, Origin: Bundesarchiv-Filmarchiv

Double saut périlleux (II), France 1899, Prod: Lumière, Length: 16 m, b&w, Origin: CNC – Archives françaises du film

Dr Macintyre's X-Ray Cabinet, Great Britain c1909, Prod: Unknown, Length: 3 m, b&w, Origin: Scottish Screen Archive

Dr Macintyre's X-Ray Film, Great Britain 1896/c1909, Prod: Unknown, Length: 14 m, b&w, Origin: Scottish Screen Archive

L'Éclipse du soleil en pleine lune [fragment], France 1907, Prod: Star-Film, Dir: Georges Méliès, Length: 41 m, b&w, Origin: Lobster Films

Écriture à l'envers, France 1896, Prod: Lumière, Length: 15 m, b&w, Origin: CNC – Archives françaises du film

Effeti di un razzo, Italy 1911, Prod: Itala Film, Length: 42 m, b&w, Origin: Deutsche Kinemathek

Les Effets du melon, France 1906, Prod: Pathé, Dir: Charles Lucien Lépine, Length: 35 m, b&w, Origin: Deutsche Kinemathek

Das eitle Stubenmädchen, Austria 1908/10, Prod: Saturn-Film, Dir: Johann Schwarzer, Length: 64 m, b&w, Origin: Filmarchiv Austria

En avant la musique, France 1907, Prod: Pathé, Dir: Segundo de Chomón, Length: 34 m, stencil-coloured, Origin: CNC – Archives françaises du film

L'Équilibre impossible, France 1902, Prod: Star Film, Dir: Georges Méliès, Length: 24 m, b&w, Origin: Lobster Films

[Erotische Filmfragmenten: Adoration érotique], Length: 30 m, tinted, Origin: EYE Film Institute Netherlands

[Erotische Filmfragmenten: Topless exotiques], Length: 30 m, tinted, Origin: EYE Film Institute Netherlands

Erreur de porte, France 1904, Prod: Pathé / S.C.A.G.L., Dir: Ferdinand Zecca, Length: 35 m, Origin: Filmarchiv Austria

Excelsior!, France 1901, Prod: Star Film, Dir: Georges Méliès, Length: 38 m, b&w, Origin: Lobster Films

Explosion of a Motor Car, Great Britain 1900, Prod: Hepworth, Dir: Cecil M. Hepworth, Length: 30 m, b&w, Origin: BFI National Archive

Extirpation d'un kyste du corps thyroïde, France 1898/1903, Prod: Eugène-Louis Doyen, Length: 80 m, b&w, Origin: Cinemateca Portuguesa

Extirpation d'une tumeur du testicule, France 1898/1903, Prod: Eugène-Louis Doyen, Length: 19 m, b&w, Origin: Cinemateca Portuguesa

Fâcheuse méprise, France 1905, Prod: Pathé, Dir: Anonymous, Length: 18 m, b&w, Origin: Cinematek – Cinémathèque royale de Belgique

Les Filles de Loth, France c1925, Length: 179 m, b&w, Origin: CNC – Archives françaises du film

Fix's Hôtel-Abenteuer [series of 10 pornographic Magic Lantern slides], b&w, Origin: Private collection Bernd Scholze

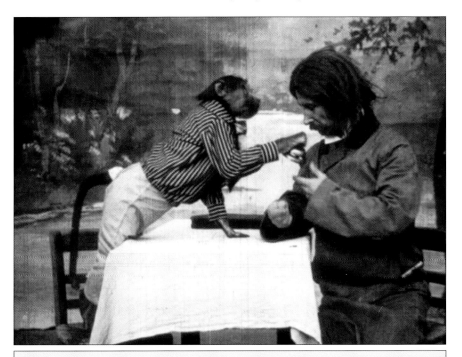

Upper: Le Singe "August" (France, 1904).

Lower: Extirpation d'une tumeur du testicule.

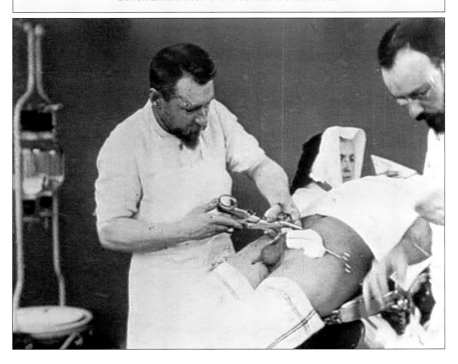

Fox terriers et rats, France c1902, Prod: Parnaland, Length: 30 m, b&w, Origin: Filmoteca de Catalunya

Fronleichnamsprozession in Trier, Germany 1909, Prod: Marzen, Edison's Elektrisches Theater im Lokale des Central-Theaters, Trier, Lenght: 52 m, b&w, Origin: Bundesarchiv-Filmarchiv

Fütterung von Riesenschlangen, Germany 1911, Prod: Komet Film, Length: 48 m, b&w, Origin: EYE Film Institute Netherlands

Große Cavalcade zu Luxembourg 1905 / Cavalcade à Luxembourg 1905, Luxembourg 1905, Prod: Marzen, Edison's Elektrisches Theater, Length: 37 m, b&w, Origin: CNA Luxembourg

Großer Blumen-Corso 1906 / Fête des Fleurs 1906, Luxembourg 1906, Prod: Marzen, Edison's Elektrisches Theater, Length: 56 m, b&w, Origin: CNA Luxembourg

Große Springprozession 1906 / La Procession Dansante d'Echternach 1906, Luxembourg 1906, Prod: Marzen, Edison's Elektrisches Theater, Length: 83 m, b&w, Origin: CNA Luxembourg

Der Hausarzt, Austria 1908-1910, Prod: Saturn, Dir: Johann Schwarzer, Length: 125 m, b&w, Origin: Filmarchiv Austria

Un Homme de tête, France 1898, Prod: Star Film, Dir: Georges Méliès, Length: 19 m, b&w, Origin: Lobster Films

L'Homme mystérieux, France 1910, Prod: Pathé, Length: 111 m / 130 m, Origin: BFI National Archive / Cinémathèque française

L'Homme qui marche sur la tête, France 1909, Prod: Pathé, Dir: Anonymous, Length: 83 m, tinted, Origin: EYE Film Institute Netherlands

Horrible fin d'un concierge, France 1903, Prod: Pathé, Length: 24 m, b&w, Origin: CNC – Archives françaises du film

[Hunde-Theater], France c1907, Prod: Pathé, Dir: Anonymous, Length: 77 m, b&w (tinted title card), Origin: Österreichisches Filmmuseum

Hurdle Jumping by Trained Dogs, USA 1899, Prod: American Mutoscope and Biograph Company USA, Length: 30 m, b&w, Origin: EYE Film Institute Netherlands

Une idylle sous un tunnel, France 1901, Prod: Pathé, Dir: Ferdinand Zecca, Length: 15 m, b&w, Origin: Filmoteca Española

L'Illusionniste double et la tête vivante, France 1900, Prod: Star Film, Dir: Georges Méliès, Length: 22 m, Origin: Lobster Films

Jubileusz 3-lecia klubu sportowego "Victoria" w Czêstochowie [fragment: *Athlete Rupprecht*], Poland c1910, Prod: Odeon Czêstochowa, Length: 23 m, b&w, Origin: Filmoteka Narodowa

"King" and "Queen", the Great High Diving Horses, USA 1899, Prod: American Mutoscope and Biograph Company USA , Length: 13 m, b&w, Origin: EYE Film Institute Netherlands

Les Kiriki, acrobates japonais, France 1907, Prod: Pathé / S.C.A.G.L., Dir: Segundo de Chomón, Length: 60 m, hand-coloured, Origin: Lobster Films / Cinémathèque française

Kobelkoff, France 1900, Length: 28 m, b&w, Origin: Lobster Films

Leap Frog, Great Britain 1900, Prod: Bamforth Company, Dir: James Bamforth, Length: 24 m, b&w, Origin: BFI National Archive

Leben und Treiben auf dem Viehmarkt am 5. Mai. Bekannte Trierer Handels-Typen im Wirken, Germany 1909, Prod: Marzen, Edison's Elektrisches Theater im Lokale des Central-Theaters, Length: 28 m, b&w, Origin: Bundesarchiv-Filmarchiv

Let me dream again, Great Britain 1900, Prod: G. A. Smith, Dir: G. A. Smith, Length: 21 m, b&w, Origin: BFI National Archive

Lèvres collées, France 1906, Prod: Pathé, Dir: Anonymous, Length: 45 m, b&w, Origin: Filmarchiv Austria

Les Maçons, France 1905, Prod: Gaumont, Dir: Alice Guy, Length: 39 m, b&w, Origin: Cinematek – Cinémathèque royale de Belgique

Madame Babylas aime les animaux, France 1911, Prod: Pathé, Dir: Alfred Machin, Length: 133 m, b&w, Origin: Lobster Films

Das malerische Luxemburg / Le Luxembourg pittoresque, Luxembourg 1912, Prod: Félix Medinger, The Royal Bio Comp., Luxembourg, Length: 99 m, b&w, Origin: CNA Luxembourg

Mary Jane's Mishap or, Don't Fool with the Paraffin, Great Britain 1903, Prod: G. A. Smith, Dir: G. A. Smith, Length: 76 m, b&w, Origin: BFI National Archive

Les Mésaventures d'un cycliste myope, France 1907, Prod: Pathé / S.C.A.G.L., Dir: Georges Hatot, 111 m, b&w, Origin: Cinematek – Cinémathèque royale de Belgique

Miss Harry's femme serpent, France 1911, Prod: Pathé, Dir: Anonymous, Length: 54 m, stencil-coloured (tinted title card), Origin: Cinematek – Cinémathèque royale de Belgique

Mousquetaire au restaurant, France 1920, Length: 150 m, b&w, Origin: Lobster Films

[Der neue Behandlungsstuhl], France c1915, Prod: Eugène-Louis Doyen, Dir: Anonymous, Length: 49 m, b&w, Origin: Bundesarchiv-Filmarchiv

Nouvelles luttes extravagantes, France 1901, Prod: Star Film, Dir: Georges Méliès, Length: 45 m, b&w, Origin: Lobster Films

Les Œufs de Pâques, France 1907, Prod: Pathé, Dir: Segundo de Chomón, Length: 39 m, stencil-coloured, Origin: Deutsche Kinemathek

Oktav-Prozession 1911 / Procession de l'Octave 1911, Luxembourg 1911, Prod: Hubert Marzen, Parisiana, Luxembourg, Length: 55 m, b&w, Origin: CNA Luxembourg

On doit le dire, France 1918, Prod: Pathé, Dir: O'Galop, Length: 127 m, b&w, Origin: CNC – Archives françaises du film

A Peace of Coal, Great Britain c1910, Length: 77 m, tinted, Origin: EYE Film Institute Netherlands

La Peine du talion, France 1906, Prod: Pathé, Dir: Gaston Velle, Length: 95 m, stencil-coloured, Origin: Lobster Films

Photographie d'une étoile, France 1906, Prod: Pathé, Dir: Anonymous, Length: 32 m, b&w, Origin: Filmarchiv Austria

La Poule phénomène, France 1905, Prod: Pathé, Dir: Ferdinand Zecca, Length: 61 m, Origin: Cinematek – Cinémathèque royale de Belgique

Premier prix de violoncelle, France 1907, Prod: Pathé / S.C.A.G.L., Dir: Anonymous, Length: 55 m, b&w, Origin: Lobster Films

Première sortie d'une cycliste, France 1907, Prod: Pathé, Dir: Anonymous, Length: 86 m, b&w, Origin: Cinematek – Cinémathèque royale de Belgique

[Pumpstation für Radfahrer], France 1906, Prod.: Pathé, Dir: Anonymous, Length: 40 m, b&w, Origin: Filmarchiv Austria

Le Réveil de Chrysis, France c1897/99, Prod: Pathé, Dir: Anonymous, Length: 15 m, b&w, Origin: Filmoteca de Zaragoza / Filmoteca Española

Le Réveil d'un monsieur pressé, France 1900, Prod: Star Film, Dir: Georges Méliès, Length: 20 m, b&w, Origin: Lobster Films

Le Roi des Dollars, France 1905, Prod: Pathé / S.C.A.G.L., Dir: Segundo de Chomón, Length: 34 m, stencil-coloured, Origin: EYE Film Institute Netherlands

Saïda a enlevé Manneken-Pis, France 1913, Prod: Belge Cinéma Film, Dir: Alfred Machin, Length: 145 m, b&w, Origin: Cinematek – Cinémathèque royale de Belgique

[S.A.R. Marie-Adélaïde au cinéma], Luxembourg 1912, Prod: Félix Medinger, The Royal Bio Comp., Luxembourg, Length: 13 m, b&w, Origin: CNA Luxembourg

Le Satyre Casimir, France c1930, Length: 104 m, b&w, Origin: Lobster Films

Sauts périlleux (I), France 1899, Prod: Lumière, Length: 16 m, b&w, Origin: CNC – Archives françaises du film

Sauts périlleux par deux (III), France 1899, Prod: Lumière, Length: 17 m, b&w, Origin: CNC – Archives françaises du film

[Scène Pornographique], France 1909, Length: 28 m, b&w, Origin: CNC – Archives françaises du film

Die Schlangentänzerin, Germany 1909, Prod: Projektions-AG Union, Length: 30 m, b&w, Origin: Deutsche Kinemathek

Sculpteur moderne, France 1908, Prod: Pathé, Dir: Segundo de Chomón, Length: 116 m, stencil-coloured, Origin: Österreichisches Filmmuseum

TOM POUCE SUIT UNE FEMME

Le Singe "August", France 1904, Prod: Pathé, Dir: Anonymous, Length: 70 m, b&w, Origin: CNC – Archives françaises du film

Les Six Sœurs Dainef, France 1902, Prod: Pathé, Dir: Anonymous, Length: 55 m, hand-coloured, Origin: EYE Film Institute Netherlands

Spiders on a Web, Great Britain 1900, Prod: G.A. Smith, Length: 4 m, b&w, Origin: BFI National Archive

St. Willibrordus-Feierlichkeiten zu Echternach 1906 aka *Übertragung der Reliquien des hl. Willibrod in die Basilika*, Luxembourg 1906, Prod: Marzen, Edison's Elektrisches Theater, Length: 25 m, b&w, Origin: CNA Luxembourg

[Street Scenes in Saarbrücken], Germany 1909, Length: 91 m, b&w, Origin: BFI National Archive (Joseph Joye Collection)

The Strenght and Agility of Insects, Great Britain 1911, Prod: Kineto, Dir: F. Percy Smith, Length: 114 m, b&w, Origin: BFI National Archive

Sur les remparts de Luxembourg / On the Ramparts of Luxembourg, France c1919, Prod: Pathé Revue, Length: 33 m, stencil-coloured, Origin: La Cinémathèque de Toulouse

The Tale of the Ark, Great Britain 1909, Prod: Alpha Trading Company, Dir: Arthur Melbourne Cooper, Length: 107 m, b&w, Origin: BFI National Archive

That Fatal Sneeze, Great Britain 1907, Prod: Hepworth Manufacturing Company, Dir: Lewin Fitzhamon, Length: 106 m, b&w, Origin: BFI National Archive

The ? Motorist, Great Britain 1906, Prod: Paul's Animatograph Works, Dir: Walter R. Booth, Length: 54 m, b&w, Origin: BFI National Archive

Théâtre de Hula-Hula, c1917, Length: 55 m, b&w, Origin: Danish Film Institute

Le Thermomètre de l'amour, France 1906, Prod: Pathé / S.C.A.G.L., Dir: Anonymous, Length: 31 m, b&w, Origin: Cinematek – Cinémathèque Royale de Belgique

Die Thronbesteigung der Kronprinzessin Maria-Adelheid von Luxemburg / Fêtes de l'avènement de S.A.R. la Grand-Duchesse Marie-Adelaïde de Luxembourg, Luxembourg 1912, Prod: Félix Medinger, The Royal Bio Comp., Luxembourg, Length: 88 m, b&w, Origin: CNA Luxembourg

To Demonstrate How Spiders Fly, Great Britain 1909, Prod: Kineto, Dir: F. Percy Smith, Length: 27 m, b&w, Origin: BFI National Archive

Tom Pouce suit une femme, France 1910, Prod: Pathé, Dir: Anonymous, Length: 113 m, b&w, Origin: BFI National Archive (Joseph Joye Collection)

Les Tulipes, France 1907, Prod: Pathé, Dir: Segundo de Chomón, Length: 88 m, stencil-coloured, Origin: Cinematek – Cinémathèque royale de Belgique

The Twins' Tea Party, Great Britain 1896, Prod: Paul's Animatograph Works, Dir: R.W. Paul, Length: 10 m, b&w, Origin: BFI National Archive

[Unter dem Mikroskop. Larve der Wasserfliege], Great Britain 1903, Prod: Charles Urban Trading Company, Dir: Francis Martin Duncan, Length: 23 m, b&w, Origin: Filmarchiv Austria

Unterschenkelamputation, Germany c1903, Prod: Messter's Projection, Length: 68 m, b&w, Origin: IWF Wissen und Medien

[Upside-Down Boxers], Great Britain 1899, Prod: British Mutoscope and Biograph Company, Dir: Anonymous, Length: 10 m, b&w, Origin: EYE Film Institute Netherlands

Upside Down: or, The Human Flies, Great Britain 1899, Prod: Paul's Animatograph Works, Dir: R.W. Paul, Length: 23 m, b&w, Origin: BFI National Archive

Voyage autour d'une étoile, France 1906, Prod: Pathé, Dir: Gaston Velle, Length: 145 m, b&w, Origin: Lobster Films

Weibliche Assertierung, Austria 1908/1910, Prod: Saturn-Film, Length: 70 m, b&w, Origin: Deutsches Filminstitut – DIF

Will Evans, the Musical Eccentric, Great Britain 1899, Prod: Warwick Trading Company, Length: 20 m, b&w, Origin: BFI National Archive

CONCLUSION

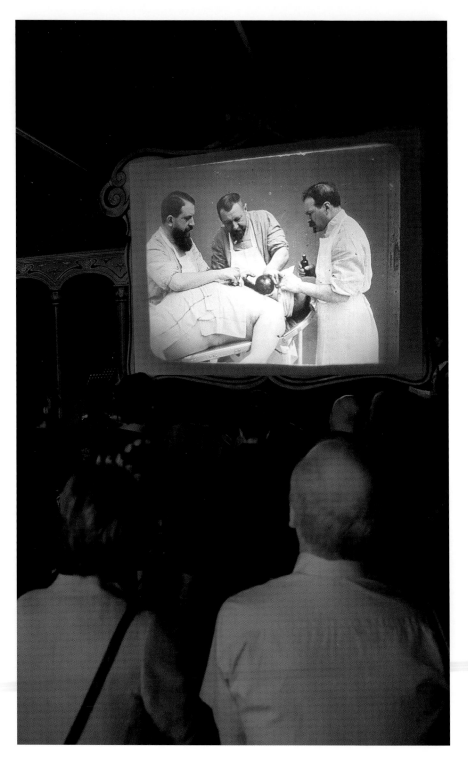

Frank Kessler

Programming and Performing Early Cinema Today: Strategies and *Dispositifs*

Since the foundation of the *KINtop* yearbook in 1992, the presentation of early films to audiences today has continued to be an important issue for the editors. Over the past two decades we (Sabine Lenk, Martin Loiperdinger and myself) have organised a series of programmes in collaboration with, among others, the film museums in Frankfurt, Düsseldorf and Munich, the Arsenal in Berlin or the Kino 46 in Bremen, but also the Cinémathèque de la ville de Luxembourg (the latter cooperation resulting in the *Crazy Cinématographe* initiative). From attempts to recreate the build-up of an early cinema screening to more didactic presentations on, for instance, the relationship between film and the Magic Lantern, but also combinations of avant-garde films from the 1920s to the 1990s, these programmes have tried to find a way to make contemporary audiences appreciate moving images from the period around 1900 as something other than "primitive" curiosities from another age.

In addition to, and sometimes also in connection with these screenings, *KINtop* regularly invited scholars and archivists to reflect on their own or their institution's activities and experiences in this area.[1] In spite of the obvious differences between them with regard to the objectives, the means, the strategies or the target audiences of these projections, a number of similarities can be observed, which in the first instance are linked to the specific status of early films.

Bridging the gap, marking the difference

Above all, and maybe self-evidently, there seems to be a shared conviction that showing films from the period around 1900 to present-day audiences, even more or less specialised ones, requires some sort of a framing that offers to the viewers a perspective on the material (nothing, of course, can guarantee that

Facing page:
EXTIRPATION D'UN KYSTE DU CORPS THYROÏDE (France 1898/1903), performed within *Dr Doyen's Surgical Cabinet* programme, in the *Crazy Cinématographe* fairground cinema tent at Luxembourg's *Schueberfouer* 2009.

the individual spectator will indeed accept this offer, as one can always adopt an alternative attitude towards the images shown).[2] This is due to the fact that, when early films are being shown today, those presenting them need to take into account the profound *difference* of animated photographies or, to use a term suggested by André Gaudreault and Denis Simard, their *extranéité*.[3] Gaudreault and Simard use this latter expression, because according to them early cinema is not 'strange' (*étrange*), but rather 'alien' (*étranger*), which leads them to declare: "Early cinema is irreducibly alien to the cinema that followed it, and it is also irreducibly alien to us, who are spectators watching it at a different time".[4]

This twofold alien-ness not only concerns scholars of film history, who always need to be aware of the fact that their object of research should not be 'naturalised' by looking at it from the viewpoint of institutionalised narrative cinema. This issue is even more important when one programs such films for contemporary viewers. Non-specialised audiences, in particular, may indeed more often than not experience the alien-ness of early cinema simply as strangeness, because the filmic forms appear 'primitive' compared to modern ones. This clearly has consequences for the way in which programmes of films from that period can be presented. Their alien-ness, on the one hand, needs to be attenuated to some degree in order to make possible an appreciation by the spectators, and on the other hand it needs to be foregrounded to some degree, for otherwise they will indeed be viewed as primitive forerunners of a cinema to come. So while having to try and bridge the gap between the cinema of today and the views and scenes from around 1900 in order to make the latter accessible, it is also necessary to mark the difference to prevent simplistic assimilations to the larger traditional story of how film developed from 'an infant state' to a 'mature art form'.[5]

At a more conceptual level it can be useful to address early cinema's alien-ness in terms of *dispositifs*. This latter term, suggested in the 1970s by the French theorist Jean-Louis Baudry to describe the relation between screen, projector and spectator in a movie theatre is generally translated into English as 'apparatus' (hence the expression 'apparatus theory').[6] As I have argued elsewhere, I find it useful to keep the original French term, not only because it more explicitly connotes the idea of a specific arrangement or disposition, but also in order to mark the shift from a psychoanalytical approach to spectatorship to one that frames the relation between the film, the viewer and the viewing context rather in terms of a historical pragmatics.[7] From this point of view one can indeed state that the so-called cinema of attractions constitutes a *dispositif* that is almost diametrically opposed to the one described by Baudry and taken to be characteristic of classical narrative cinema.

In addition, such a change of perspective allows taking into account the fact that there is not simply one cinematic *dispositif* (as Baudry's theory is often read), but that throughout the history of animated photography, both synchronically and diachronically, a large variety of *dispositifs* have co-existed and continue to do so. Thus, for instance, and to stay within the realm of early cinema, screenings in vaudeville or variety shows, in fairground tents, in town halls and in nickelodeons, all provided rather diverse viewing contexts for moving pictures and by the same token they can be described as so many different *dispositifs*. Consequently, each of them can be said to have produced its own pragmatic framework within which audiences experienced animated views. So, again, even for the period up to the First World War there is not just one *dispositif*, which can be defined in opposition to the one of classical narrative cinema, but quite a range of them, allowing for a much more nuanced approach. Consequently, the main point here is not so much an identification and definition of *dispositifs* in terms of historically attested practices with the goal to establish some kind of a taxonomy, but rather a perspective on these practices in terms of *dispositifs*, using the concept more modestly as a heuristic tool to investigate the manifold ways in which the various types of moving images (including also home movies or the many forms of what Rick Prelinger called "ephemeral films")[8] were presented to audiences. The aim of such studies, then, is to understand the complex interaction between texts, viewers, and viewing situation (including also aspects of technology and institutional framings) in a given historical context.

Thus, to begin with, there just simply is no all-encompassing *dispositif* of early cinema, which could be used as a normative model for archival or museological reconstructions. And, obviously, even in cases when it is possible to trace and bring together all the films shown in a historically attested programme, it would be an illusion to presume that anything only remotely like the historical experience could be retrieved. The *dispositifs* of archival or museological screenings, per definition, function in a profoundly different way, as they have to both bridge and mark the historical gap.

Dispositifs of archival and museological screenings

When looking at the various reflections on the archival and museological practices to organise screenings of early films for audiences today, these quite evidently aim at serving a twofold purpose. On the one hand, they pursue a didactic or scholarly project of providing a framework for today's spectators to appreciate these films as historical objects, that is with regard to their original viewing context, their functions and what they may have meant to their audience at the time. On the other hand, such screenings also want to offer a specific aesthetic experience, which is obviously different from the one viewers are used to nowadays when going to the movies, but which for that very reason should give them a new and unexpected kind of pleasure. One possible strategy here is to create an environment that evokes the period around 1900, so that audiences are, as it were, prepared for a different kind of viewing experience (as does, for instance, the *Crazy Cinématographe*), Both dimensions are generally intertwined, and there are different ways through which these aims may be achieved.

An important point, though, is the goal to make possible a positive appreciation of early films. In this respect the practices of archival and museological screenings today differ from the ones presented in a traditional teleological perspective with their emphasis on the way in which the "primitive" films foreshadowed the art of a cinema that blossomed from the 1920s onwards. So while underscoring certain of their qualities, such earlier programmes did frame the productions from the turn of the century up to the 1910s as being not yet capable of reaching the aesthetic and formal standards that were established by the masterpieces of the later silent period. Even more radically, as Ansje van Beusekom has shown, the avant-garde movements in London, Paris or Amsterdam in the 1920s programmed 'pre-war' films mainly in order to point toward the difference between these outdated and ridiculous specimens from a bygone era and the current state of the art.[9] Even though these screenings did in fact pursue something like an educational or didactic purpose, they did so by using the films from the past as negative examples allowing to appreciate the artistic progress made since.

In order to offer audiences a possibility to experience early films in a more positive way, archives and museums need to provide them with a different kind of context, and also to address them in a different way. To begin with, the fact that such institutions organise screenings with the goal to provide both instruction and pleasure to their audiences of course not only is valid for presentations of early films. More in general, watching a film at a film museum or at an archival film festival is an experience that differs profoundly from simply going to the movies to see a recent release, because there is at least in principle always something like a tacit assumption that there is some kind of purpose to such a show. In accordance with the larger cultural function of these institutions, the viewer presupposes an intentionality, which then can be stated explicitly (in programme notes, announcements, introductions etc.) or remain an implicit presupposition. At the same time (and this is where the strategies developed in recent years with regard to early cinema differ from the traditional presentations, and especially from those organised by the avant-garde circles mentioned above), the (re-)discovery of a historical film or film programme is also meant to give pleasure to the audience. In this respect, that is in the combination of these intentionalities, the archival or museological *dispositif* is quite different from the one that is dominant in mainstream moviegoing.

So, taking up the term discussed earlier, for early cinema this means that its alien-ness should be appreciated as such, on its own terms. In order to achieve this, curators and programmers use various strategies of contextualisation, ranging from the reconstruction of historical viewing conditions (knowing of course, that the historical experience as such cannot ever be retrieved) to the creation of specific new environments into which the historical films are embedded. This concerns, by the way, also other forms of distribution such as DVDs, in which case the contextualisation is provided by means of various paratexts. Giovanna Fossati and Nanna Verhoeff have termed this the "chaperone model" where "archives present film programs as *selections* made by the archive that holds the film, often with the use of explanatory titles or with an accompanying catalogue, which explain (and justify) the archive's choice and contextualize the films either historically or aesthetically".[10] To this, one can add that also the programming strategies themselves are part of the model (and of the *dispositif*).

Contextualisation through information

In a thoughtful essay on the rediscovery and programming of early non-fiction films in the mid-1990s, starting with a workshop at the Amsterdam Film-museum in 1994 and a retrospective organised by the Giornate del Cinema Muto in 1995, Stephen Bottomore discusses the problems of making accessible these films to an audience today, even one composed of archivists and schol-ars.[11] Apart from advocating a programming strategy that would rather follow the historical practice of mixing genres instead of confronting viewers with a series of similar films (in this case non-fiction views), he also engages with the approach the Amsterdam Filmmuseum chose. The participants of the work-shop viewed the films without receiving contextual information about them, because, as Bottomore puts it, the aim was to "stimulate scholarly reactions to these rarely seen reels, in areas such as the visual style and technique of individual films and variation/evolution between films".[12] For Bottomore, the shortcomings of such an "aesthetic approach" are that in the end it does not help to fully understand the potential complexity of early non-fiction.

> As well as helping in identification, extra information really is vital in better appreciating non-fiction films (and here I would definitely part company with the 'aesthetic school'). Indeed it can sometimes be the only way of giving signification or importance to otherwise dull and meaningless pieces of celluloid held by film archives.[13]

This experience has undoubtedly been shared by many who, confronted with views of landscapes, crowds, streets, factories etc. that in themselves presented little visual attraction, discovered the richness of the material thanks to the information provided by titles, catalogue descriptions, introductory presenta-tions or comments during the screenings. In fact, depending on the type of films being shown, these various ways to provide contextual information may even vary in their efficiency. From the elaborate composition of reels with views by the Mutoscope and Biograph Company compiled by Nico de Klerk of the Amsterdam Filmmuseum with only minimal information as an example how a predominantly aesthetic approach can in fact be almost self-sufficient, to Vanessa Toulmin's extensive explanations accompanying the screenings of Mitchell & Kenyon films at the Giornate del Cinema Muto, there are many precedents of successful presentations of early non-fiction. In 2010 those attending both the Domitor conference in Toronto and the Cinema Ritrovato Festival in Bologna could make an interesting comparison when the same material, the expedition film shot by Vittorio Sella for the Duke of Abruzzi's 1909 expedition trying to climb the K2, was shown. In Toronto there was an introduction to the programme with ample contextual information about the historical background of the footage, which was then shown accompanied by a piano. For the audience, however, it proved to be difficult to link the information provided beforehand to the images that were projected. In Bologna the historian, Giovanni Lasi, not only introduced the films, but also provided comments during the screening, based on the texts used at the time for the illustrated lectures about the expedition. While individual appreciations of either presentation may vary, in this case at least it is quite clear that in Bologna the audience could discover more in the various views because the explanations given helped to orient the spectator's gaze. However, with a different kind of footage such additional information might be experienced as redundant, superfluous and even distracting.

Nevertheless, it is quite obvious that giving contextual information and offering a historical framing of early films generally is one of the most important aspects of the archival and museological *dispositif*. The forms in which this is done may differ considerably, yet no one would deny that this is indeed a fundamental and important task for the organisers of such screenings.

Contextualisation through defamiliarisation

When arguing in favour of mixed programmes emulating the structures of the early period instead of adopting the model of the retrospective organised around a single theme, Bottomore evokes the example of the concert hall: "[…] a concert has to be carefully programmed to attract and hold an audience. The most popular programme would probably combine a variety of different styles and composers."[14] Bottomore uses this example to underscore his point that generic diversity is more appropriate for early cinema programming than homogeneity, but does so presuming that the films presented date from more or less the same period. However, as Karola Gramann and Heide Schlüpmann point out, one of the amazing, yet characteristic features of concert programmes lies in the fact that they can quite easily combine a Baroque flute concerto with a Brahms piano piece and a composition by Busoni.[15] In their own work with students at Frankfurt University, Gramann and Schlüpmann had them present combinations of short films from different periods, the common denominator then being the limited length and the fact that, in relation to mainstream cinema practices today, the short format as such is marginalised. So here the alien-ness of the films from the period before the First World War is to some extent neutralised by the contact with another type of films that for today's audiences also represents an out-of-the-ordinary viewing experience. In this respect, the contextualisation here functions as a defamiliarisation, because the early films are no longer seen simply as embryonic forms of the narrative feature films but as examples of short films as a distinctive aesthetic practice.

In a similar fashion a programme compiled by *KINtop* that toured in Germany in 2001 and 2002 combined a series of views from the early period with avant-garde films from the 1920s to the 1960s. In contrast with the aforementioned strategies adopted by the avant-garde associations in the 1920s and 1930s that used the "pre-war" films to underscore the difference between their own artistic work and the commercial productions from a bygone era, *KINtop* rather focused on the way in which such a framing could open up the visual richness of the early films to 21st century viewers. The link between early cinema and later avant-garde films was in fact established already by Tom Gunnings famous essay "The Cinema of Attractions. Early Film, Its Spectator, and the Avant-Garde", as well as in the writings of Noël Burch.[16] As Jan-Christopher Horak points out in quite some detail, the experimentations with movement, speed, light and the cinematographic technology in general that one finds in many films from around 1900, can be linked to similar filmic strategies in the avant-garde movements in later years.[17]

The *KINtop* programme *Alles dreht sich, alles bewegt sich* (taking up the title of an experimental film by Hans Richter) not only tried to establish such a connection between early and later avant-garde films, but also to offer a contextualisation of the former allowing to perceive them in a new way. The idea, however, was not to establish them as "forerunners" of the avant-garde, but rather to have the audience look at them from a much more uncommon angle. The frame of reference now being not the institutionalised narrative cinema, but the much more marginalised experimental forms, viewers could experience them in a different manner. With a horizon of expectation oriented towards already defamiliarising avant-garde practices, and thus towards non-conventional cinematic modes, the alien-ness of early cinema was no longer a mark of "primitiveness", but could be perceived as just another kind of unorthodox filmmaking.

In both these examples, contextualisation does not aim – or at least not in the first instance – at an embedding of early films within the exhibition practices of their time, nor do they seek to convey historical background information as their main goal (while of course leaflets and introductions to the screenings did offer this to quite some degree, certainly in the *KINtop* programmes). The *dispositif* in these cases did not imply that the spectators were addressed first and foremost in a didactical manner. The organisers proposed instead an aesthetic contextualisation that, as it were, defamiliarised the alien-ness of early cinema to a second degree, by creating a connection with other films that do not correspond to mainstream cinema. This strategy was then meant to reduce early cinema's alien-ness, or to make it at least graspable as a mode of filmmaking that is different rather than "primitive".

Contextualisation through dislocation and spectacle

The programming strategies discussed above, whether foregrounding historical information or aesthetic contrast, are generally embedded within the familiar institutional frameworks of archives, film museums, festivals, university film clubs or specialised movie theatres. Some initiatives, however, have chosen to take the screening out of such spaces and try to make audiences encounter early films unexpectedly or under unexpected circumstances. This is the case for the *Imaginaire en contexte* events organised by Eric de Kuyper for, and together with, the Belgian film archive in cooperation with various other institutions, and also the *Crazy Cinématographe* shows at the Luxemburg *Schueberfouer* fair and elsewhere.[18] Such screenings are always, and consciously, anachronistic, as they explicitly seek to provoke an unexpected encounter of a contemporary audience with historical films. An encounter that is conceived in such a way that the spectators can, and actually should, experience it as an *event*.[19]

The films, in both cases, are but one part of this experience. The music, the set-up, the environment – a cemetery, a painter's studio, or an exhibition hall for de Kuyper's screenings, the tent on a modern fairground for the *Crazy Cinématographe* – are essential ingredients for these spectacles. For the fairground show, two actors performing as both barkers and lecturers play an important role as mediators between the audience and the images. They appear as reminiscences of the historical presenters of fairground shows and at the same time as their modern variant, their interventions being of course of a rather different nature as they include filmographic and other historical background information.[20] Although to some extent at least the films may be considered the main focus of the show, the *Imaginaire en contexte* as well as the *Crazy Cinématographe* screenings could be said to rather function as something like a *Gesamtkunstwerk*. Here the archival and museological *dispositif* is indeed acted out as a performance, as an attraction in its own right. In fact, as the lecturers are played by actors and the texts are delivered according to a fixed script, which is repeated during every show, the screenings literally are performances.

Of course, there have been several initiatives of a similar kind inside and outside Europe. As examples one could name *The Living Nickelodeon* by Rick Altman and his colleagues, trying to recreate the experience of American moving picture shows around 1905–1910 or the reconstructions of the 1906 *Ouimetoscope* presentations in Quebec organised by Germain Lacasse together with the Cinémathèque québecoise. Here, as is the case with the Luxemburg initiative, showmanship plays an important role. The performers have to captivate the audiences and create a mood that makes possible an appreciation of the films. What distinguishes the *Crazy Cinématographe*, as well as these North American initiatives from the *Imaginaire en contexte* events, is that the former all have their point of reference in historical practices, the ultimately unbridgeable gap notwithstanding. The special events organised by Eric de Kuyper and the Cinémathèque royale de Belgique, however, have no pretensions in this direction. They leave the traditional *dispositifs* of film projections behind and completely dislocate the screenings into a completely different type of performance.

So on the one hand, leaving the traditional archival or museological context, such initiatives either create spectacular encounters with early films within a *dispositif* that refers to, or evokes, a historical mode of presentation, while at the same time being aware of the fact that the experience will differ radically from this historical precedent. On the other hand, the dislocation can even go further, creating a form of spectacle that cannot be referred to any screening practice that may have existed in the past. In all cases, however, the contextualisation does give a framework to the films that in a way neutralises their alien-ness as they become part of a spectacle that, as such, does not resemble the habitual experience of going to the movies.

Conclusion

For more than two, maybe even three decades now, audiences all over North America, Europe and on other continents as well, have had an increasing number of occasions to encounter moving pictures made about a century earlier. While sometimes still presented as "primitive" curiosities that could only fascinate the "naïve" spectators of their time (in spite of all the scholarly efforts, the "train panic myth", for instance, is still around and repeated *ad nauseam* by programmers, journalists and sometimes even film historians), more and more often the organisers of screenings reflect on how they can not only do historical justice to the films, but also turn them into an attraction for audiences today. Even though, once again, the "death of cinema" is being proclaimed as digital images conquer our media environment, animated photographies from the years around 1900 can work their magic in many and sometimes unexpected ways. The films do need a contextualisation, sometimes in the form of a confrontation, to be appreciated, and archivists, festival curators, scholars and other organisers of such screenings have explored a broad range of possibilities to provide this. Maybe one of the most interesting aspects of this development is that scholarly rigour and showmanship are not mutually exclusive. Quite on the contrary, historical research in fact produces the very basis upon which the acts of showmanship can be performed. And from time to time someone, who is known as a meticulous researcher, a grave academic, or a scrupulous archivist, may even be seen as a performer, standing next to a screen or sitting behind a piano, trying to share with an audience her or his fascination for the animated photographies that enchanted the public a century ago.

Notes

1. See Livio Jacob, "Arbeiten für den stummen Film. Die Geschichte der Cineteca del Friuli und der Giornate del Cinema Muto in Pordenone", *KINtop* 3 (1994): 195–199; Dominique Païni, "Der frühe Film zwischen Zufall und Bühne", *KINtop* 5 (1996): 150–154; Frank Roumen, "Die neue Kinemathek. Ein anderer Ort, ein anderes Publikum, eine andere Zeit", *KINtop* 5 (1996): 155-159; Karola Gramann and Heide Schlüpmann, "Die Kunst des Filmezeigens – Kurzfilm und frühes Kino in der universitären Lehre", *KINtop* 11 (2002): 159–164; Ivo Blom, "Eine Reise um die Welt vor 90 Jahren, or: The Travelling Showman Revisited", *KINtop* 12 (2003): 151–164; Eric de Kuyper, "Der Stummfilm der ersten Jahrzehnte – Studiengegenstand oder Schauobjekt", *KINtop* 14/15 (2006,):137–150 (for an English version of de Kuypers text see elsewhere in this volume).

2. To give an example: a film museum can for instance organise a screening of hand- or stencil-

Frank Kessler

coloured trick films in order to demonstrate to their audience the amazing visual and attractional qualities of such productions, making use maybe even of a lecturer highlighting these features, whereas someone with a particular scholarly interest might focus on other aspects, trying even to block out the framing discourse provided by the institution.

3. See André Gaudreault and Denis Simard, "L'extranéité du cinema des premiers temps: bilan et perspectives de recherche" in Thierry Lefebvre and Michel Marie (eds), *Les vingt premières années du cinéma français* (Paris: Presses de la Sorbonne Nouvelle, 1995), 15–28.

4. Ibid., 22 (my translation).

5. One might add that whoever teaches film history faces a similar task when dealing with the early period.

6. See for the English translation Jean-Louis Baudry, "The Apparatus – Metapsychological Approaches to the Impression of Reality in the Cinema" in Philip Rosen (ed.), *Narrative, Apparatus, Ideology* (New York: Columbia University Press, 1986), 299–318.

7. See Frank Kessler, "The Cinema of Attractions as *Dispositif*" in Wanda Strauven (ed.), *The Cinema of Attractions Reloaded* (Amsterdam: Amsterdam University Press, 2006), 57–69.

8. See Patrick Vonderau, "Vernacular Archiving. An Interview with Rick Prelinger" in Vinzenz Hediger and Patrick Vonderau (eds), *Films That Work. Industrial Film and the Productivity of Media* (Amsterdam: Amsterdam University Press, 2009), 51–61.

9. See Ansje van Beusekom, "'Avant-guerre' and the International Avant-garde. Circulation and Programming of Early Films in the European Avant-garde Programs in the 1920s and 1930s" in Frank Kessler and Nanna Verhoeff (eds), *Networks of Entertainment. Early Film Distribution 1895–1915* (Eastleigh: John Libbey, 2007), 285–294.

10. Giovanna Fossati and Nanna Verhoeff, "Beyond Distribution: Some Thoughts on the Future of Archival Films" in *Networks of Entertainment*, 333 (emphasis by the authors).

11. Stephen Bottomore, "Re-discovering Early Non-Fiction Film", *Film History* 13.2 (2001): 160–173.

12. Ibid., 166.

13. Ibid., 167–168.

14. Ibid., 165.

15. See Gramann and Schlüpmann, 159.

16. See the reprint of Gunning's essay in Strauven (ed.) and Noël Burch, *Life to those Shadows* (London: BFI, 1990).

17. Jan-Christopher Horak, "Auto, Eisenbahn und Stadt – frühes Kino und Avantgarde", *KINtop* 12 (2003): 95–119.

18. See de Kuyper in *KINtop* 14/15 and in this volume, as well as Claude Bertemes, "Cinématographe Reloaded. Notes on the Fairground Cinema Project *Crazy Cinématographe*" in Martin Loiperdinger (ed.), *Travelling Cinema in Europe* (Frankfurt am Main / Basel: Stroemfeld, 2008), 191–218, and also Claude Bertemes and Nicole Dahlen in this volume.

19. This of course is in itself an anachronism, as historically, of course, the screening of these films did not have the character of an event.

20. See also Stephen Bottomore, "Workshop Review", *Early Popular Visual Culture* 9.1 (2011): 87–90.

The Contributors

Madeleine Bernstorff lives in Berlin and works as a film curator, researcher and teacher in the fields of film, art, and documentary. She is a member of the Programming Committee of the International Short Film Festival Oberhausen since 2000. Recent projects include *Early Interventions: Suffragettes – Extremists of Visibility*, in collaboration with Mariann Lewinsky, and *Iceploitation* – a collaborative project with a group of artists from Tromsø, Norway, leading to an exhibition, fanzine, film programme, seminar and an intervention at the Polar Museum. www.madeleinebernstorff.de

Claude Bertemes is director of the Cinémathèque de la Ville de Luxembourg. In 2007, he launched the fairground cinema project *Crazy Cinématographe*. He received his PhD in Communication Studies from the University of Münster. He served on the Executive Committee of FIAF (International Federation of Film Archives) and was FIAF's Deputy Secretary General from 2003 to 2005. Since 2010, he is a member of the Executive and Artistic Committee of Discovery Zone – Luxembourg City Film Festival. He has been a member of the Script Reading Committee of the *Luxembourg Film Fund* from 1999 to 2008. He has co-edited the restoration of the German version of LOLA MONTES. His publications on media entertainment, film art and visual heritage include *Traumhaus, Musée du cinéma et 'Digi-cinéphilie'* (forthcoming).

Nicole Dahlen is project manager at the Cinémathèque de la Ville de Luxembourg. She coordinates the fairground cinema project *Crazy Cinématographe* since 2006. She received her Master in Communication and Cinema Studies from the University of Liège and the Sorbonne Nouvelle, Paris. Since 2010, she is also in charge of the educational programming of Discovery Zone – Luxembourg City Film Festival. She performed for several theatre and dance companies in Paris. In 2007, she founded her own dance theatre company *Trotz Ensemble*, for which she serves as artistic director.

Tom Gunning is the Edwin A. and Betty L. Bergman Distinguished Service Professor in the Department of Cinema and Media at the University of Chicago. He is the author of *D.W. Griffith and the Origins of American Narrative Film* (University of Illinois Press) and *The Films of Fritz Lang; Allegories of Vision and Modernity* (British Film Institute), well as over hundred articles on early cinema, film history and theory, avant-garde film, film genre, and cinema and modernism. With André Gaudreault he originated the influential theory of the "Cinema of Attractions". In 2009 he was awarded a Andrew A. Mellon Distinguished Achievement Award, the first film scholar to receive one and in 2010 was elected to the American Academy of Arts and Sciences. He is currently working on a book on the invention of the moving image.

Andrea Haller is a film historian and curator at the German Film Museum in Frankfurt. In 2009, she received her PhD from the University of Trier for a study on programming strategies and female cinema audiences in Imperial Germany. She has published various articles on local film history, the history of cinema programming and of cinema audiences and the relations between cinema, fashion and modernity. Her recent publications include "Film, Fashion and Female Movie Fandom in Imperial Germany" in *Not so Silent. Women in Cinema before Sound* (Stockholm 2010)

Frank Kessler is professor of Media History at Utrecht University. His main reseach interests lie in the field of early cinema and the history of film theory. He is a co-founder and co-editor of *KINtop*, the German yearbook of early cinema. From 2003 to 2007 he was the president of DOMITOR, an international association to promote research on early cinema. Together with Nanna Verhoeff he edited *Networks of Entertainment. Early Film Distribution 1895–1915* (John Libbey, 2007).

Eric de Kuyper is a Belgian writer, critic, filmmaker and film scholar. He created the Film and Performance Studies Programme at the University of Nijmegen and acted as Deputy Director of the Netherlands Filmmuseum from 1988–1992. He was the co-founder of the Dutch cinema studies journal *Versus* and has contributed to numerous international periodicals such as *Communications*, *Cinémathèque*, *KINtop*, *Semiotica*, or *Film History*. De Kuyper is the author of a book on the director Alfred Machin and co-editor of a collection of essays on Asta Nielsen. Over the past years he conceived and curated several programmes involving early films, such as the *Imaginaire en contexte* series for the Cinémathèque royale de Belgique or *Vom Meeresgrund* (together with Mariann Lewinsky) for the Oberhausen Short Film Festival.

Mariann Lewinsky is film historian and curator of film programmes and restoration projects. She lives in Zurich. Since 2004, she is director of the programme series *A Hundred Years Ago* – a film history in films for the festival Il Cinema Ritrovato in Bologna.

Martin Loiperdinger is professor of Media Studies at the University of Trier and a co-founder and co-editor of *KINtop*, the German yearbook of early cinema. He was Deputy Director of the German Film Institute – DIF from 1993 to 1997. He covered film and cinema history in television features on German newsreels, the Federal Film Archive of Western Germany, the Lumière Brothers, film pioneer Oskar Messter, advertising film and the German avantgarde, and on the history of colour film. He published books and numerous articles on film propaganda and on early cinema history. He is editor of

Celluloid Goes Digital (2003), and of *Travelling Cinema in Europe* (2008), and co-editor of *Geschichte des dokumentarischen Films in Deutschland* (2005). Recently, in collaboration with Ludwig Vogl-Bienek, he curated the DVD SCREENING THE POOR 1888–1914 (Edition Filmmuseum, 2011).

Dick Tomasovic is Associate Professor in history and aesthetics of cinema and performing arts at the University of Liège. He makes videos, writes fictional works and develops projects for the stage. His publications include *Le Palimpseste noir, notes sur l'impétigo, la terreur et le cinéma américain contemporain* (Yellow Now, 2002), *Freaks, la monstrueuse parade de Tod Browning* (Cefal, 2006), *Le Corps en abîme, sur la figurine et le cinéma d'animation* (Rouge Profond, 2006) and *Kino-Tanz. L'art chorégraphique du cinéma* (P.U.F, 2009).

Vanessa Toulmin is Director of the National Fairground Archive, Professor of Early Film and Popular Entertainment, and Head of Cultural Engagement at the University of Sheffield She is co-editor and founder of the *Journal of Early Popular Visual Culture* and was joint-coordinator of the BFI's Mitchell and Kenyon Project. With her wide range of numerous publications, variety shows, and public lectures, she is a leading authority on Victorian entertainment and screen culture. Her publications include *Electric Edwardians. The Story of the Mitchell & Kenyon Collection* (Bfi publishing, 2006).

Picture credits

Cinémathèque de la Ville de Luxembourg (cover, 78, 87, 90, 98, 106, 136)
Collection Fondation Jérôme Seydoux-Pathé (25, 27)
Cineteca di Bologna - Archivio fotografico (29, 33, 46, 47)
EYE - Film Institute Netherlands (31, 38, 39, 48, 61, 62, 63, 95, 111)
Lobster Films (49, 121 lower, 125 lower)
Cinematek - Cinémathèque royale de Belgique (82, 85, 110, 114, 121 upper)
Filmoteca de Catalunya (83)
Filmoteka Norodowa (91)
Cinemateca Portuguesa (101, 129 lower)
Danish FilmInstitute (114)
Deutsche Kinemathek - Museum für Film und Fernsehen (117 upper, 125 upper)
CNC - Archives françaises du film (117 lower, 129 upper)
All other credits are given with the illustrations themselves.

KINtop

KINtop Jahrbuch zur Erforschung des frühen Films
KINtop Schriften

The **KIN**top yearbook was founded in 1992 by Frank Kessler, Sabine Lenk, and Martin Loiperdinger to familiarise German readers with the growing body of important international work on early cinema. Some of the articles were published in English in order to address readers elsewhere, too. Among the contributors or translated authors there were many prominent scholars in the field such as Richard Abel, Stephen Bottomore, Noël Burch, Elena Dagrada, Monica Dall'Asta, Thomas Elsaesser, André Gaudreault, Tom Gunning, Mariann Lewinsky, Charles Musser, Heide Schlüpmann, or Vanessa Toulmin, as well as numerous young researchers presenting their work. In 1993 the first volume of **KIN**top Schriften was published, a series of monographs and anthologies on pioneers such as Ottomar Anschütz, Oskar Messter, and Ludwig Stollwerck (who brought the Lumière Cinematograph to Germany), but also on other subjects including travelling cinema, detective serials, exotic views, or the collection of early films screened by the Swiss Jesuit Abbé Joye. In addition, **KIN**top organised many screenings and film programmes in Germany, and was involved in several exhibitions related to the early period.

With this new series **KIN**top *Studies in Early Cinema* published by John Libbey the editors of **KIN**top would like to contribute to the thriving field of early cinema studies on an international level.

KINtop Jahrbuch zur Erforschung des frühen Films
KINtop Schriften

Stroemfeld Verlag: Frankfurt am Main and Basel www.stroemfeld.de

KINtop Websites at Trier University

www.kintop.uni-trier.de

www.kintop_studies_in_early_cinema.uni-trier.de

Contact: kintop@uni-trier.de

KINtop Schriften in English

Martin Loiperdinger (ed.): *Travelling Cinema in Europe. Sources and Perspectives* (KINtop Schriften 10), Frankfurt am Main / Basel: Stroemfeld, 2008.

English Contributions in KINtop 1 (1992) – 14/15 (2006)

Barnes, John; Fletcher, Tony; Vries, Tjitte de: *Arthur Melbourne-Cooper – Discussion 4* (1995): 169–180.

Blankenship, Janelle: *"Leuchte der Kultur" – Imperialism, Imaginary Travel and the Skladanowsky Welt-Theater* 14/15 (2006): 37–51.

Blom, Ivo: *Eine Reise um die Welt vor 90 Jahren*, or: *The Travelling Showman Revisited* 12 (2003): 151–164.

Bottomore, Stephen: *"Devant le cinématographe". The Cinema in French Fiction (1896–1914)* 13 (2004): 93–110.

Carrozza, Tiziana: *The Eye Over the Hill. Aerial Photography up to the First World War* 3 (1994): 117–128.

Chabria, Suresh D. G.: *Phalke and the Méliès Tradition in Early Indian Cinema* 2 (1993): 103–115.

Gray, Frank; Vries, Tjitte de; Donaldson, Geoffrey; Slide, Anthony: *Arthur Melbourne-Cooper – Discussion Continued* 5 (1996): 177-189

Gunning, Tom: *A Quarter of a Century Later: Is Early Cinema Still Early*? 12 (2003): 17–31.

Hogenkamp, Bert: *The Impact of Audiovisual Media in the Town of Utrecht. A Research Project at the University of Utrecht* 9 (2000): 117–129.

Hogenkamp, Bert: *De Lichtstraal, the organ of the Dutch Union of Theatre and Cinema Employees (1916–1921)* 14/15 (2006): 127–135.

Humphries, Martin: *From a Crumbling Ruin to the Workhouse. How the Cinema Museum came to be established* 7 (1998): 177–182.

Jung, Uli; Roll, Stephanie: *Women Enjoying being Women. Some Observations on the Occasion of a Retrospective of Franz Hofer's Extant Films in Saarbrücken* 8 (1999): 159–168.

Kessler, Frank: *"Fake" in Early Non-Fiction* 14/15 (2006): 87–93.

Klerk, Nico de: *What the Papers say – The case of the film-related papers of Jean Desmet* 14/15 (2006): 113–121.

Komatsu, Hiroshi: *Moving Images on the Screen before Cinema in Japan* 7 (1998): 153–162.

Meade, Allen: *All in the Day's Work* (1910) 11 (2002): 11–14.

Rossell, Deac: *The Public Exhibition of Moving Pictures before 1896* 14/15 (2006): 169–205.

Schulze, Brigitte: *D.G. Phalke's Raja Harischandra in British India of 1913. Pioneering a National Cinema Under Colonial Rule* 3 (1994): 173–189.

Schulze, Brigitte: *Tracing Living Histories of Cinema in Nasik. Reflections on a Sociology and Archeology of Early Indian Cinema* 6 (1997): 185–192.

Söderbergh Widding, Astrid: *Hasselblads Fotografiska AB as Film Producer 1915-1917. Sensationalism or Quest for Quality?* 9 (2000): 151–165.

Solomon, Matthew: *The "National"/"Nation" and Early Cinema – Report on the 2006 Domitor Conference* 14/15 (2006): 221–225.

Toulmin, Vanessa: *The Importance of the Programme in Early Film Presentation* 11 (2002): 19–33.

Tsivian, Yuri: *Cutting and Framing in Bauer's and Kuleshov's Films* 1 (1992): 103–113.

Vries, Tjitte de: *Arthur Melbourne-Cooper, Film Pioneer Wronged by Film History* 3 (1994): 143–160.

Vries, Tjitte de: *Arthur Melbourne-Cooper (1874–1961). A Documentation of Sources Concerning A British Film Pioneer* 13 (2004): 146–176.